Jordie Albiston has published eight poetry collections, and a handbook on poetic form. Two of her collections (*Botany Bay Document* — retitled *Dreaming Transportation* — and *The Hanging of Jean Lee*) have been adapted for music-theatre: both enjoyed recent seasons at the Sydney Opera House. Jordie works within formal boundaries: traditional, experimental, or self-imposed. She seeks the musical cadence while endeavouring to exact a mathematical sense of existence. Often she utilises archival sources from which to wrest a kind of documentary cataloguing; other times she refers to an internal witness of experience. Her poetics are highly charged with vertigo, and doubt. Jordie's work has won a number of awards, including the Mary Gilmore Award and the NSW Premier's Prize. She lives in Melbourne.

T0099245

Jordie Albiston
Jack & Mollie (& Her)

UQP

First published 2016 by University of Queensland Press
PO Box 6042, St Lucia, Queensland 4067 Australia

uqp.com.au
uqp@uqp.uq.edu.au

Cover design by Sandy Cull, gogoGingko
Author photograph by Melody
Typeset in 11.5/14 pt Adobe Garamond by Post Pre-press Group, Brisbane
Printed in Australia by McPherson's Printing Group, Melbourne

Cataloguing-in-publication data
is available at http://catalogue.nla.gov.au

ISBN 978 0 7022 5418 5 (pbk)
ISBN 978 0 7022 5787 2 (epdf)
ISBN 978 0 7022 5788 9 (epub)
ISBN 978 0 7022 5789 6 (kindle)

University of Queensland Press uses papers that are natural, renewable
and recyclable products made from wood grown in sustainable forests.
The logging and manufacturing processes conform to the
environmental regulations of the country of origin.

for
the girl
&
the boy

Pray tell me, sir, whose dog are you?

—Alexander Pope

J had never been owned by a dog   did
not become a dog ownee until the
age of forty   enter Jack   his full name
—what monosyllabic moniker can
adequately sum up or represent

such a complex & multi-layered being
as a dog?—was Our Brother Jack (comma)
Kerouac (full stop)   with name-dropping nods
to the expat Aussie novelist &
San Francisco Superbeat   however

putting such frivolous pretensions &
appellative tongue-twisters aside   Our
Brother Jack (comma) Kerouac (full stop)
quickly & thankfully became known quite
simply as Jack   Jack is watching her now

as she writes at a quarter to five in
the morning   Mollie of course is nowhere
to be seen   *I am having the watch of*
Her   even though it is the blackness &
we should be at sleep   Mollie is dream-dream

but it has never been for Mollie to
have the watch of Her   my eyes have the want
to go backwards   but I keep them look by
having the jerk of my head   I must do
the stay   this is of the significant

duty   at least she is not having the
wet-face or doing the go-around all
in the no-light   at least she is something
of happy   & Boss Dog is not of the
maximum size   Mollie did not arrive

1

until Jack was four   two kennel moves &
a leash of life changes later than where
this story begins   thus you—dear Reader—
must linger for her rambunctious rock-rol-
licking & ready-for-anything *yip!*

🐕

J was unwell for some time before her
Edisonesque event   her marriage had
ended   her children had somehow transformed
from infants into teens   she was somewhat
alone & she simply wanted something

to love   many of these months remain mud
in her mind but she still remembers this
impulse   something to love   & then the light
switched on & her heart was lit & she saw
it up there   the Dog Star   *she is not with*

the very well when she comes to pick me
up   she holds me too squash   even with the
worry-worry I do the sad & bold
goodbye to mother   brother   gather my
self for what next   I have the comprehend

I will not be return   I have too the
comprehend that I can love Her   that I
will love Her   that love will have all of the
everything good in the end   J had done
her fieldwork   she was allergic to cats

despite their apparent attraction to
her   appearing out of nowhere at friends'
houses   on streets   in parks   to slide around
her legs   take up residence on her lap
appraise her approvingly with other-

worldly eyes   she could not warm to them   cats
are regal independent pleasingly
aloof   yes   but up close   first the sneezing
second the itching & finally the
complete inability to see   J

did not dislike mogs   she just could not bear
them   thus prominent on her Pooch Research
List—perchance this particular matter
applied to dogs—was Non-Allergenic
Breed   to the AKC Information

Site! 'single-coated' 'non-shedding' 'dander'
a whole new lexicon   a whole canine
planet   Maltese   Bichon Frise   Portuguese
Water Dog   Peruvian Inca   o
lordy!   to the sea for a think!   & there

sitting on a rock on the sand   minding
her business   dangling her toes   it came
upon her   quick as a vision   slow as
a dream   poking his nose right at her knee
The Dog She Knew She Could Love   swallowing

her customary compulsion she spoke
to the bloke at the end of the leash &
enquired as to the pup's pedigree   Er
Aussie Terrier   he gruffly replied
while gazing out above her head at a

pair of fluorescent bikinis   the hound
was smallish   exuding autonomy
companionship & everything nice as
he calmly tolerated her gaze   he
was beautiful in a rugged kind of

way   no cutesy-wutesy namby-pamby
here   coat not too short not too long   bluish-
black shot through with tan   face strong & alert
eyes dark & keen & intelligent—o
those doggy adjectives!—ears upright &

vigilant   J was smitten   there & then
she knew this was the dog for her   knew she
wanted the dog to be male   & for some
whacky reason she knew that somewhere   a-
waiting her   was a little man named 'Jack'

🐕

local paper   *The Age   The Trading Post*
the supermarket noticeboard   J searched
& searched   but to cut a long story short
as they say (or in this case several
longish months into one shortish sentence)

she finally located a litter
of four Australian Terrier pups
(huzzah!) on the very far side of large
Melbourne   her desire for a dog having
steadily progressed to a yearning   &

that yearning having become pure longing
she made the trip   trusty *Melway* upside-
down & unsteady on lap   requisite
$400 at the ready   but
when she arrived only two of the brood

remained   at least they were boys   how can she
describe?   a couple of fluffballs   black &
pure gorgeousness   expressing distinctly
differing temperaments   even at
only eight weeks   one was amok   jumping

& tumbling from couch to basket to floor
to basket to couch—again again—the
other just sitting   studying her face
answering her eyes   difficult to put
into words   she thinks she just stood there   can

only recall the faraway phrase   The
shy one he's called Jack   Jack?   as though in a
trance J gathered up 'Jack' & headed for
the door   she expects the seller mentioned
money   she expects she paid   he may have

proffered a profusion of detailed &
complex pup-raising hints   may have offered
the recipe for his favourite self-
saucing chocolate pudding   she has no
idea   no memory at all of

the man's face/voice/name/suburb   nor the poor
den-mum who was no doubt nearby   mourning
her imminent loss   no nothing   nothing
nothing at all   except for the fact that
she had found him   Little Man Jack!   at last

for the road trip back there was no *Melway*
on lap but a prepossessing pup called
Jack   driving along—in retrospect quite
unsafely let alone illegally
(given Jack's place just beneath the steering-

wheel)—J was consumed with a seraphic
sense of calm   she had found Her Dog!   again
unsafely   illegally   she could not
help but gaze down periodically
at this compact collaboration of

trust innocence serenity warmth   &
baby Jack just lay there—deep black eyes fixed
on hers—all the way Home   apart from one
essential deviation   The Pet Shop
yes   despite her assiduous dog-based

research over the preceding months   J
had neglected to plan ahead—whatso-
ever—in terms of the basic canine
essentials required in order to house
a pooch   she had been unwell indeed!   no

preparations at all in place   no bed
no bowl no clippers or brush no collar
or tag or leash no toys or chew-bones no
anti-flea stuff no anti-pee stuff not
even any food   thus The Pet Shop &

the only one she knew was located
deep within the local (& colossal)
shopping mall   now J could not simply leave
her new Best Friend alone in the car could
she   so pup-in-arms she fought their way to

Pet's Paradise & accumulated
the obligatory investments   (does
a dog really *need* all this?)   so much to
carry   instinctively J placed the pup
upon one of her shoulders to allow

her to ferry the vast doggy booty
& Jack seemed fine with that—happily perched
like a pirate's parrot—& thus he stayed
until they made it back to the car   o
lordy   little did J realise what

an enormous precedent had firmly
& irrevocably been set in place
right from that very first morning   well she
was a novice   she admits   & she had
hitherto never been owned by a dog

🐕

I have the much like of it up here   the
perfect sitting for a being like me   a
more fuller & safer view of the all
than the seeing down there   example   when
we go to the many-people-place   not

only will I have the all over what-
whats if travelling the way down below
but I have the understand I will be
trample   up here I have the high eyes to
identify my all-arounds   of course

I must go the way below some often
as I have the depend on the sniff to
comprehend the every   but her shoulder
is of the significant special on
account of my near-near to Her   & we

are of the similar see which from a
philosophical brings us much close   there
is more to life than feet feet feet I have
the assure   having eventually
reached Home (dog on right shoulder   arms fully

occupied with a dog's Christmas stash) J
set about the task of introducing
Jack to his new place of residence   &
to her relief—once he had snuffled each
inch & snaffled down lunch—he sent her a

look which said Satisfied   *I have much for*
the occupy with the examine &
organise of the all new mine   the toys
are joy   example   I have the instant
like to The Ball & the tiny pink-pink

with the ringing   the tartan coat has the
warm-handsome-warm & the flame-box even
of warmer   the choker does not have the
quite so joy   or the push-pull-lead   but in
the over I have the inherit of

distinct   as to the bed   well I will not
be doing the dream-dream in that one   all
comfortable & stylish I have the
concede   but never the lie-down in else-
where from Her   never for a being like me

Jack having completed a diligent
& thorough inspection of his new Home
it was time for J to attend to a
few overdue chores   Little Man followed
her everywhere   a constant miniature

shadow   trotting behind her wherever
she went   Organise washing   Attend to
dishes   Take out compost   Jack already
& always a steady four feet at the
rear   half an afternoon later—despite

his formidably focussed & super
determined persistence in tailing her—
J realised he was tired   *dog* tired   ah!
now for the inaugural road-test of
his new comfy bed!   it had been a long

& complex day after all   picking up
the exhausted pup   J gently placed him
in the quilted manger she had prepared
complete with home-knitted blanky (which had
wrapped her own babies in a former life)

a couple of cushions   a soft toy or
two   a shirt of hers which smelled—pleasantly
she trusted—of her   but nope   no go   if
anything the new bed seemed to make Jack
wake up   J tried a few more times   cooing

gently   stroking his tiny head   & yes
his breathing slowed   his eyes finally closed
& he appeared to doze while making those
angelic sweet baby sucking sounds   but
each time she stood to continue her chores

he was back on duty in an instant
escorting her every move   hmm   well she
could not discard pressing domestic &
cordon bleu concerns   so she picked up Our
Brother Jack   propped him on her right shoulder

where at last—despite an awkward clutching
of sorts—he did indeed fall asleep   *arrh*
arrh   me hearties   big mistake   even she
realised there was no going back from
here   some hours later it was time for J

to attempt sleep herself   yes the Little
Man had been untimely torn from mother
& brother   yes he had been subjected
to the psychedelic chaos of an
enormous urban shopping centre   yes

he had been unceremoniously
supplanted into a new Home   yes he
had 'assisted' with varied household tasks
(how he coped with the fumes of chopped onions
or that Domestos without wanting *Off*

shoulder! Off! is beyond her) & simply
put   his entire world had been turned upside-
down   yes she realised all of that   but
now it was time for bed   so let the fun
begin   her ablutions complete J kissed

the tiny tacker   tickled his tummy
& tucked him into his snug little bed
in its snug little lounge-room corner &
proceeded to her own room where she had
barely reached the doorway & he was there

looking up at her with those delicious
liquid eyes   no   she would not be seduced
by a two-month-old dog   Are you not tired
Little Man?   Come on   Back to bed   seven?
seventeen? twenty-seven times?   she was

not counting   & she won't subject you to
a blow-by-blow description of each firm
but polite attempt to get the guy back
into his cot   but—just for the record—
she tried   yes she did   she really really

tried   anyway   call her weak call her the
stupidest person you ever met   but
she was tired too   so she thought what the heck
his bed can be close to mine   what is the
difference   &—spent as she was—quickly

carried out a total relocation
of Jack's bedding essentials from the lounge
into her room   over by the window
next to her desk   a perfect place for a
sleepy pup   nope   no go   not a bar of

it *non* *nein* *nyet* NO! it was going to
be a long night   Jack just would not stay in
his bed   o lordy it was *hours* she swears
before she moved it adjacent to hers
whereby she could hang down one arm   her hand

on his back   & thus they would blissfully
sleep   nope   no go   even writing about
this is making her tired   anyway—long
story short again—after much fruitless
negotiating Jack ended up on

her bed   J knew this was not the correct
solution   that dogs can live for fifteen
years   but this was how things transpired   she had
had it   she was right out of ideas
yes quite with the good settled now   thank you

🐕

following Jack's arrival—three? four? five
weeks?—J was again unwell   she recalls
a room with walls made of glass   & trays &
corridors & doors   she recalls Helen
Hunt kissing Jack Nicholson   &—twice? thrice?—

her own little Jack in the hospital
garden for visits   the two of them were
overjoyed to see each other   & the
cuddles & ball-throwing & general
happy play was curative   memories

12

of Jack are clearer than those of human
callers during that time   there was no sense
of culpability or failure or
disgrace with him   & he   being Dog   had no
agenda other than to be with &

love her   in the moment   with no other
thought than the Now   no judgement no distress
no regret   lending new sense to Macbeth's
famous pronouncement 'Throw physic to the
dogs'   *I have the much sad of her gone   her*

not-there at the Home is the nearly can't
take   I am of the trouble with the dream-
dream & lose the like for the food & walk
& toys yes even The Ball   it is Boss
Dog who is of the fault   it is Boss Dog

who makes her have the go away   this is
the worry-worry for me   he is big
& I am small   but I never throw the
hope that eventually she will be
finding the way back to Home   & to me

shortly after J's return she packed up
car & picked up Jack & journeyed down to
the coast   Venus Bay is a wild stretch of
unadulterated ocean-meets-land
not at all well represented by the

13

relatively tame term 'bay'   its coast is
wide & extensive   drawing way away
into distance until obscured—in both
directions—by wave-tossed flotsam & soft
briny mist   walking this shoreline is an

inspirational exhilarating
cleansing thing   the most excellent dunes drift-
wood & kelp   the moody shape-changing hue-
changing sea   &—most important—very
very few people   happy snaps from that

holiday show Jack as inquisitive
Little Man   nose down   tail up   sniffing &
snuffling   checking out yet another New
World   there he is   all of six inches tall
a most handsome chestnut tan invading

an otherwise pitch black coat   ears far too
big for such a small face   racing along
beach   leaping to catch The Ball   already
revealing his 'ratter' instinct—*genus
terrarius*— responding to calls Go

Get It! Go On! more than any other
utterance she made (except of course his
own name)   a wonderfully overgrown
garden surrounded their temporary
Home   Jack seemed particularly taken

by flora   it being mid-summer there was
a plethora of flowers & any
in his immediate vicinity
were eye-balled snout-sniffed paw-tapped taste-tested
eaten   each morning J sat outside in

pyjamas & sun & watched Jack wander
in wonder around the yard as though it
were Eden (which it pretty much was)   on
a number of occasions—ensconced in
his methodical & meticulous

examination of daisy or shrub—
the pup was perhaps a tad too enthused
& *ker-choo!*   this event would catapult
him backwards into a brief sitting stance
before toppling him sideways into the

grass   there he lay supine for two or three
seconds—stunned by the ferocity of
his own physicality—then reclaim
an upright position   shake himself back
into doggy mode & resume his bold

exploration   these sneezes filled J with
such fits of laughter that she too almost
collapsed   happy moments are of untold
worth   utterly essential for living
on this earth   like sleep or water or air

🐕

dog & ownee visited the beach each
day   J is an unstoppable swimmer
when it comes to saltwater   regardless
of shark warnings rip warnings storms   on the
opposite side of the coin   dams—yabbies!

mud! I can't see the bottom!—& rivers—
snakes! logs! I can't see the bottom!—frighten
her   but *the sea the sea*   J would plant a
tent pole to secure Little Man & then
she was off   now Jack by nature was not

what you would call a brave boy   despite an
undeniable fervour for life he
was reticent & cautious   something of
an introvert at heart   but love it would
seem conquers all   during one of J's brief

excursions into the turbulent &
mighty rumpus so characteristic
of Venus Bay   she happened to glance back
at the beach   & in that solitary
moment was forced to digest a full-scale

drama in an eye-blink   for there stood the
tent pole   empty of tenant   & there—at
least thirty feet into the swirling white-
water—heading straight toward her through the
cacophonous ruckus of surf—was a

small black dot   *Jack*   breaker after breaker
assaulted his tiny frame   submerged his
tiny head   & with a mother's sudden
instinct J dove into immediate
& furious save-mode—*Please God! Please God!*

Let me get there in time!—endeavouring
to thrash through the football field or so of
recalcitrant swell that agitated
& churned between them   time & again she
lost sight of the Little Man as he was

dunked by a continuous onslaught of
waves   but—after what seemed much longer than
it probably was—J finally reached
Her Dog   Jack was shaking with shock & cold
& she clasped him in joy & he clung in

return as they waded back to shore   safe
on the sand   Jack wrapped in a towel   she held
him & held him until he warmed & his
tremors eventually ceased   Brave Boy
she kept saying   *Brave Boy Brave Boy Brave Boy*

when J ruminates about that day she
remains unable to comprehend the
courage   the determination   the sheer
pluck of the dog in the face of what was
undoubtedly an indescribably

petrifying experience   how had
a miniature three-month-old pup sustained
the enormous energy required to
press against such odds without succumbing
to the obvious?   love   devotion   she

can muster no other explanation
not only was Jack her companion   he
was now a warrior   a soldier   a
champion   her hero   J had not thought
her own love for this minikin being could

ever or at all expand but it did
it did   in fact her heart could contain it
only just   why do we love our dogs?   well
perhaps that discussion can wait   all J
knew at this single point in time was that

she would stand by him as he stood by her
regardless of what life threw up   after
the Venus Bay incident—& despite
the fact that *Jack by nature was not a*
brave boy—he demonstrated no fear on

subsequent sojourns to the ocean   one
is compelled to wonder if indeed he
recalls that day at all   *I do not have*
the much remember   only for the smash-
smash & the under & the knowledge that

I must not be of the letting Her leave
from my eyes again   not off with Boss Dog
or into the many-people-place or
the anywhere that I am not   never
with the not-look   ever-ever again

Venus Bay a good few weeks behind them
Jack was five months old when a second life-
threatening incident occurred   this time
the Little Man would *never* forget &
scars from that day were forever scored on

his innocent sweet doggy soul   as J's
health continued to improve she & Jack
ventured on longer & more frequent walks
or   as she & Jack ventured on longer
& more frequent walks J's health continued

to improve   the latter is probably
closer to the truth for—left to her own
devices—J most certainly would have
stayed shuttered from the world at this stage of
her recovery   again Jack excelled

as her one & only true physician
in that he forced her out of the house by
default & into the open air   with
Home as the obvious starting point there
were a number of walking routes from which

she always allowed the pooch to choose—left
right up down over around—which way shall
we go today?   & what a production
it was   initially Little Man would
conduct a full accomplished forensic

investigation of the small front yard
& nature strip   nosing & sniffing the
usual spots in order to discern
All's Well With The World before coming to
a considered standstill at the base of

the driveway   from there he would examine
each direction in turn & then hold his
head high (well as high as it could go) to
carefully sample the various wafts
of olfactory information &

late-breaking canine news when—all of a
sudden—they were off!   other times J drove
them to a park or piece of bushland a
bit further afield   Diamond Creek with its
fragrant surrounds was a favourite   bird-

song & wildflowers in summer & a
mystical foggy hush in the cold   Jack
proved a wonderful companion in
terms of exploration   together—the
Little Man off-leash—they would muck about

down by the water   sidestepping through stiff
regal bullrushes   rock-hopping great rounds
of flat grey stone   climbing the overgrown
banks of grevillea   acacia   &
Victoria's state floral emblem pink

heath   enjoying nature's beatific
gifts   this particular day however
was a Street Walk Day   having completed
the perfunctory observations &
computations Jack finally made a

decision   his tail curled back on itself
in anticipation & joy   it was
a sunny late autumn afternoon &
as they perambulated J thought Life
Is Good   now   how long had it been since that

thought had tapped on the door of her mind   let
alone gained access?   but those were the words
that came—unbidden & unforced—*Life Is
Good*   in retrospect she should have heard those
old alarm bells clanging away (for we

must never take even the smallest thing
for granted) but she did not   she was too
busy savouring the feeling behind
those three unassuming words   then less than
a block from Home it occurred   abruptly

out of nowhere & with no warning two
dogs—a smallish white bitsa & (far more
disturbingly) a largish black Pit-Bull
cross—appeared on the opposite side of
the road   unleashed & unaccompanied

they came hurling themselves in a dervish
of maniacal gnashing & savage
snapping across the bitumen toward
little Jack & herself   being a fair way
off adulthood Jack was still wearing a

small red harness instead of a collar
for walking   this was a godsend in that—
without conscious thought & with pure instinct—
J immediately tossed the pup up
in the air   whereby she swung him around

her head like a lasso   yelling   with Jack
momentarily safe from those two sets
of hellishly furious jaws   it was
obviously Jack the dogs were after
& as a result J was not bitten

as such (though she was repeatedly clawed
in their rabid attempts to seize the air-
borne Little Man)   alerted by her screams
three men—plumbers as she would later learn—
similarly appeared out of nowhere

& shovels in hand began whacking at
the frenzied dogs   completely unfazed the
animals continued with their attack
& so—while one of the plumbers grabbed J's
arm & swiftly removed woman & dog

to the nearby worksite—the other two
men persisted with their counter-attack
unfortunately to no effect   'their'
plumber had no sooner sat her-clutching-
Jack-clutching-her down

when the Pit-Bull materialised yet
again   with admirable astuteness
their guy lunged towards her   grabbed Jack   & threw
him into the back of a ute   slamming
shut the shiny black cover   & all three

men resumed their whacking (what on earth does
it take to deter a Pit-Bull?) until
finally finally the brutal beast
desisted & slunk away   mission in-
complete   as J violently shook &

the plumbers—almost as violently—
panted   they looked at one another in
disbelief   not a sentence having been
exchanged   J opened her arms as Jack was
retrieved & she saw that—apart from shock—

the pup had indeed incurred a couple
of injuries   bleeding from both back &
leg   (though the multifarious scratches
J herself had received were instantly
visible   it was not until the next

morning that bruises began to flourish
& bloom   darkly blushing across shins &
thighs like an oriental vine or clouds
before a storm)   as shocking an event
as they had just experienced   it was

nothing new from an historical point
of view   words discovered in 66
AD on a mosaic Pompeii floor &
attributed to Petronius read
quite simply 'Cave Canem' (Beware of the

Dog)   *I will never have the forget of*
that day   the smell & yell   the blue-blue-blue
of the sky rounding round   no   I will not
have the forget   I will carry that day
with me wherever the where I go   as

I have the must   because behind that tree
because around that corner   before you
know & all of the sudden   I must keep
the look   & just in case   I will never
have the forget   forever for that day

🐕

although J informed the council of what
had occurred &—after much door-to-door
searching—the authorities located
the (unregistered) perpetrators   she
declined her right to have the plumbers act

23

as witness   make a report   see those dogs
put down   she should have perhaps   but she just
could not   she simply ascertained that the
by-laws be abided   & that the two
animals be appropriately tagged

& restrained   as for the Little Man   well
he was never the same again   something
was taken from him that day   something which
would remain unrecovered   something deep
& primal & absolutely central

to his wellbeing   something strangely like what
the lion in *The Wizard of Oz* had
lost   *his courage*   Life Is Good?   yes   repeat
after me in your nicest & loudest
voice   *Life Is Good   Life Is Good   Life Is Good*

🐕

over the following weeks Our Brother
Jack grew   & not just his body but his
hair   & it grew   & it grew   finally
when he was about eight or nine months old
J became decidedly wary   for

where was the handsomely rugged Aussie
Terrier she was expecting him to
become?   where was The Dog She Knew She Could
Love from the beach?   Jack was beginning to
appear   well   a tad *feminine* she thought

not that a feminine-looking male posed
a problem in itself   she was merely
flummoxed   was Jack a throwback of sorts?   had
his recent trip to the vet left him not
only neutered but sexually dis-

oriented?   okay   alright   don't get
your knickers in a knot   so   back to the
trusty internet   typing in the key
words 'Australian' & 'Terrier'   as
often as not J found the term 'Silky'

interjected between the two   with some
curiosity & not without some
trepidation she held her breath & clicked
on a site &—surely a mistake—there
he was   o dear   no   it couldn't be   with

greater curiosity & even
greater trepidation she selected
another site & clicked & there he was
again   Jack   her Jack   again & again
& again   J removed her glasses   cleaned

the lenses on her jeans rubbed her eyes re-
focussed   Jack   an Australian SILKY
Terrier   how had this happened?   for months
she had searched for Aussie Terrier pups
she had searched & searched & she had found   but

as she instantly & clearly saw   the
seller from whom she had purchased Little
Man had obviously neglected to
include the word 'Silky' in his other-
wise well-worded advertisement   what was

she to do?   hire a private detective
to somehow track down this guy (no cogent
memory of name or phone or address)
& politely request a refund?   hey
no not that   she loved her dog   she *loved* him

                    🐕

trawling through site after Silky site   J
became ever-increasingly alarmed
for not only was Jack's coat vexingly
long at this still-adolescent stage   it
was set to become—that's right!—a whole lot

longer   J was absolutely stunned at
the photos she encountered featuring
adult Australian Silkies   to her
these dogs looked nothing less than completely
& utterly farcical   a surreal

amalgam of Dougal from *The Magic
Roundabout*   the hairy-faced Chewbacca
of *Star Wars* fame   & a bright-eyed Kewpie
Doll   not only did their coats all but reach
the actual ground   the hair on their heads

was—horror upon horror—*tied up in
a top-knot*   no no no   there was no way
this was going to happen   not to Our
Brother Jack (comma) Kerouac (full stop)
not to Little Man   not to Her Dog   *No!*

in both Jack's & her own defence—he a
dog & she a novice ownee—J was
altogether unaware of the sheer
volume of certified canine breeds whose
ludicrous appearances far exceed

that of the Silky   relegating it
to nothing short of subtle!   indeed—as
she felt compelled to ask more than once—what
is *wrong* with the person who must go to
such time-consuming money-consuming

fundamentally & astoundingly
questionable lengths in order to
produce the most fundamentally &
astoundingly questionable types
of dog?   a top-knot is relatively

tame as a 'feature' she assures you   just
take a cursory glance at some of the
excessively extravagantly un-
usual dog-types On Show   anyway
further reading confirmed what J would have

preferred to consider a bad rumour
or joke but was forced to concede in due
course   *Jack was one of them*   she fixated
on a couple of facts   'The coat is five
to six inches long'   (hey! that's longer than

his current height!)   'The coat consists of fine
shiny hair very prone to tangles &
matting unless recurrently groomed'   at
this point J permitted herself a nice
glass of wine   & took herself off to bed

*I do have the appreciate for the
big & the small of categories &
their have to   but this is me under the
discuss   she has not positioned her eyes
on me or conducted the stroke of my*

*back all this light-time   that alone is hard
to have the accept   but I conserve of
the hope that at the complete of day the
names & words & terms make the good for me
because I am what I am what I am*

okay   it's only outward facades we're
talking about   not something major like
personality   lovability
or Dog (she means God) Forbid   genetic
weakness   it's just looks—style fashion coiffure—

these things change alter come & go all the
time   they mean nothing!   at least he's healthy
(twenty claws twenty toes)   at least he is
happy   & as J read more & more   it
began to make a strange amount of sense

                    🐕

the Australian Silky Terrier
was developed by crossing the Yorkshire
('Yorkie') & Australian Terrier
with perhaps a gene or two of the Cairn
& Skye thrown in   this breeding project took

place as the nineteenth century closed some-
where in Sydney   the Silky weighs eight to
eleven pounds & grows to a height of
nine to ten inches   feet are small & cat-
like   litter size generally three to

four   lifespan normally twelve to fifteen
years   the dog is classed as 'Terrier' in
Europe but 'Toy' in Australia   (eek!
other recent & humiliating
discoveries aside   J Did Not Have

A Toy Dog)   to continue   a Silky's
nature is characterised by innate
intelligence (J was convinced Jack could
actually read her mind at times) &
courage (the Venus Bay incident)   it

is happiest when physically close
to its master (the right shoulder) (the bed
situation)   this dog bears suspicion
toward strangers (a number of meetings
requisite before Jack would accept a

newcomer without barking) & strange dogs
(Puppy School was a disaster) & will
usually attach itself to one
person alone (singular devotion
yes)   the Silky is sensitive to sound

& will easily scare (Jack would flee to
one of his Safety Zones—behind toilet
or under bed—at hearing anything
on his Personal Aural Phobia
List   thunder   fireworks   backfiring cars   trains

Bob Dylan   braying possums   rattling keys
contraltos   food processors   the Channel
Nine news music   sneezes   running water
scrunching paper   lawnmowers   Philip Glass
hysterical weeping   hysterical

laughing   the Apple Mac trash noise   falling
leaves   et cetera)   the Silky dislikes
being treated as anything other than
an equal (Jack absolutely refused
to use the expensive doggy-door J

had installed & insisted entering
& exiting the 'people' door just like
her) (Jack would sit nowhere in the car but
the passenger seat even if someone
was already there) (on a number of

occasions J woke in the morning to
find Jack's head on the other pillow—at
the exact same level as her own—calm
as a clam—while she shot like a rocket
out of the bed   & landed on the floor)

at last J fully & immutably
accepted the fact she had herself an
Australian *Silky* Terrier &
she bore no regret whatsoever   she
even learned to love Jack's shiny & black

satin coat   though she kept it trimmed to a
civilised length (*Hairy Maclary From
Donaldson's Dairy* was an enormous
improvement on the Dougal/Chewbacca/
Kewpie-Doll visage)   & most important

of all there was decidedly & most
definitely no top-knot   as for Jack
the little dog laughed to see such sport   *I
have the great proud to pass of the test &
show my happy I am! I am! I am!*

well   what can be said?   life continued as
it is prone to do   & a routine—both
predictable & productive—governed
the hours at Home   weekdays J wrote   with Jack
either watching-her-watching-the-screen or

dozing at/on her feet   she endeavoured
to keep Saturdays & Sundays word-free
(although poems did not always heed said
schedule) & practiced flute or listened to
music or tended the yard   Little Man

always in tow   routine is good for one's
health & so it was for J   mostly the
black kept itself at bay   mostly it stayed
away   but not (no not) completely   *I*
do not have the understand why she has

the wet-face so many   why she holds me
too squash in the no-light   I do not have
the know for the people condition   I
do the attempt to keep Her with the dry-
face   it is the duty of me   to stay

with the smile   catch-catch of The Ball   make Boss
Dog go of the minimum size   because
she has the depending on me for the
happy   & the happy is the big &
significant of my job   throughout the

evenings ball-tossing did not function
merely as distraction from difficult
things   but a very real source of fun   Jack's
unrelenting enthusiasm for
retrieval   & his obvious joy in

the activity was an excellent
panacea for the sick at heart   ball
held aloft J would throw it as far as
the fence permitted & Jack would Go Get!
with the unfettered fanaticism

of any zealot   Little Man's antics
caused much pain-assuaging laughter as he
conducted his own search party of one
in ever-increasing concentric arcs
from where he believed The Ball had come to

rest   attuned to that unappealing-to-
humans-wet-blanket-tennis-ball odour
Jack was—more often than not—successful
in his quest   when unsuccessful he would
dig or climb or crawl or whatever it

was the situation required until
frustration   at the very last   got the
better of him   he would then return to
her empty-jowled with the most literal
of hang-dog looks   if perchance The Ball came

to rest in the ancient in-ground swimming
pool Jack simply gave up on the spot   There's
no way I'm getting in there   *You* threw it!
You get it!   ball-tossing in one of the
nearby parks was carried out on a much

grander scale   with the aid of what she's sure
will go down in doggy history as
the greatest invention of all time J
was able to launch The Ball *up into
the sky itself*   & have it land *at least*

a mile away   for a humanoid whose
ball skills were rivalled only by those of
the celluloid Lisa Simpson this was
no mean feat   her secret?   The Chucker   a
colourful neon plastic aid for the

socially-unrecognised-sportily-
challenged   moulded in the shape of a huge
shoehorn   the 'horn' replicating an ice-
cream scoop with the exact dimensions of
a tennis ball   whoopee!   okay so *she*

considered it the greatest invention
of all time as well   for not only did
The Chucker allow her—again again
& again—to amaze herself with the
longest highest & most lyrical of

ball-throwing arcs   but it also saved her
the act of touching a saliva-soaked
ball with her own skin   the abovementioned
scoop snapping itself onto The Ball with
ne'er a back-bend required   miraculous!

Jack was also pretty impressed by J
(well   The Chucker)   as long as she remained
willing to employ this apparatus
Jack remained willing to go fetch   & fetch
& fetch he did   o the tenacity

of the terrier!   never—no   never—
was it the dog who approached the human
beseeching Can we go Home now?   it was
the human—barely repressing wonder
at her newfound pitching expertise—who

had to remember & responsibly
deploy their African vet's solemn words
Little dog have chook heart   *I love The Ball*
even when I have the fatigued   or the
despondent   my only more love is Her

🐕

Jack was not only a Go-Get-It! whose
success rate went unequalled   but he was
an excellent catch as well   lithe enough
to leap at least six times his own height in
order to bring down a ball tossed from up

to thirty feet away   Superdog!   &
tennis balls were not merely for catching
or retrieving either   Jack—like J—was
a dedicated 'net-head'   &—ball wedged
in mouth—was quite partial to watching the

tennis on tele   & we're not talking
the hot-pink variety of tennis
ball here   no we are not   when following
a match the Little Man's jaws were always
ardently whole-heartedly clamped on a

yellow ball   just like those being hit back &
forth by Federer   Nadal   Djokovic
(which puts paid of course to the widely held
view that dogs are colour-blind)   another
pastime was known as 'Mister Churchill'   o

yes *Mister Churchill*   this particular
diversion was initiated by
Jack himself   wandering around—proud as
Punch—with a chew-bone ridiculously
poking sideways from his mouth J could not

help herself   Your cigar Mister Churchill
Please give me your cigar!   these sentences
accompanied by repeated lungeings
in Jack's direction   a playful pretence
at stealing his find of the moment   &

Jack would have none of it   hackles raised the
dog would begin a growl which would balloon
exponentially in intensity
with each lunge until it seemed the very
house would disintegrate from the force of

the tremors & waves   yet another loved
game of Little Man's—albeit only
in summer—was swimming in the pool   well
you couldn't really call it swimming   as
for the most part he was in J's arms   still

Jack did love a dip in January
or February on those few sizzling
days   so hot they were almost liquid in
themselves   J would swish him slowly from side
to side through the water &—lulled by the

cooling motion—the dog would fall into
a dreamy daze   eyes half closed   the faintest
of smiles across his jowl   sometimes J would
face him to the edge & release him to
paddle on his own to the steps   this was

not appreciated quite so much   scenes
of Venus Bay?   she did not know but she
did persist   as she needed the pooch to
be able to navigate his way *out*
of the pool in case he ever fell *in*

🐕

enduring the impermanence of post-
marital life   permanent Home yet to
be found   J went to live for a time in
the pre-Black Saturday mountains   The Shack
was cheap but had room enough (barely &

just) for one   unfenced & bordering the
edge of a National Park teeming with
wombats wallabies & other wildlife
native to the ranges   such a confined
living space combined with strict State laws was

not the most appropriate place for kids
or canine   this proved harder than she had
anticipated for in her new big
aloneness J found she craved the comfort
& company of Our Brother Jack more

than ever   & she missed her kids—too much!—
who were completely unable to 'fit'
in The Shack   so it was not perfect but
a kind of half-way house until she could
properly find a stable address she

might again call Home   in the meantime J
allowed the good air & the good trees to
do their good work   which they did   The Shack stood
right at the top of a twisting turning
extremely narrow fern-lined ascent   &

whilst J was relatively at ease on
this road—having lived in the region when
her children were infants—she still had to
travel cautiously   especially at
night or in fog   one would negotiate

a sharp curve only to stop face to face
with a stationary kangaroo or
bumper to bumper with another car
&—with the steepest of declines not more
than a yard or two from either side—a

lapse of concentration—at even the
slowest pace—could prove fatal   for Jack this
drive became a laborious & un-
happy thing   he would whine & cry for most
of the trip   & J could not blame it on

motion sickness vertigo grief at the
loss of daily routine or even a
sense of (simple?) displacement   no   she did
not blame any of those things   no—right or
wrong—J laid the blame squarely on the vet

🐕

as a two-year-old canine Little Man
had visited the vet a number of
times   he had been de-sexed at six months   a
problematic tooth had been removed   the
usual round of vaccinations had

occurred   & he had had his claws clipped   now
one would imagine the latter to be
the most benign of veterinary
procedures on any given list   but
this was unfortunately a long way

from the truth   indeed Jack's one & only
professional manicure had been a
brutal affair   & the dog had never
forgotten   J had not actually
requested the service (being able &

willing enough to perform the task her-
self) & the vet—having administered
the annual inoculation one
afternoon—had simply gone ahead &
done it   holding Jack down he had taken

a paw & proceeded to 'clip' each claw
by an excessive two thirds   way into
the o-so-sensitive quick   Jack's squeals had
rung loud & real as J swiped him from the
vet in speechless protest (for which the vet

upbraided her   Owner too soft   Owner
need get tough)   by the time she got Jack back
to the car her t-shirt was crimson with
blood   & by the time they returned Home the
car seat was similarly stained   beaming

Jack straight to the laundry   J dissolved salt
in a trough of warm water & submerged
the sore paws   whorls of blood continued to
snake from each affected claw for a full
twenty minutes   accompanied by Jack's

unabated yelping   such a hacking
job would have been excruciatingly
painful—a torture—as anyone who
has ever torn a nail will warrant   from
that time onward claw-clipping would prove more

than an unpleasant chore for them both   &
from that day forth Jack would begin to fret
the moment he was placed in a car   *I*
never have the like for the man-with-the-
hurt   I have the endure of the sharp   it

is over with the fast   & I do not
have the complain when I am ache in the
mouth   or when I have the stay in the cage
until light-time next   & that is the worst
part the blackness without Her   worse than the

not sleep & the soreness & the strange feel
different   even then I have the not
complain   because I have the love & the
trust   she puts my blanket & the smell of
Her there for the cage   & when we are Home

she does the hours with me & cares of me
& calms of me   with my bed in front of
the flame-box   & then she does dream-dream by
my side when the blackness comes again   there
on the floor   there by my side   those things I

have the cope for   but not when he cuts in
my paw   I do not have the understand
for that   & I do not have the like for
the noise-with-the-fast   ever or ever
in case I am having the go back there

despite such difficulties a certain
healing of a certain kind did occur
during those months on the mountain   there was
the time—for example—that J ambled
crept crawled deep into the bush & simply

sat   expecting nothing more than the bush
itself & its special secret sounds   then
after half an hour or so of moody
musings a 'peck-pecking' roused her & she
lifted her head to find a female lyre-

bird—stocky & brown—rooting for food on
the dry bush floor   as she watched a strange &
most privileged scenario began
to unfold   slowly   deliberately
like a *leitmotif* or a dance   in a

circuitous fashion a male lyrebird
was approaching   noisily shaking his
magnificent tail feathers & launching
the opening bars of his (stolen) song
with which he hoped to seduce the hen   (peck-

peck-peck)   over & over his display
of mimicry was delivered   'doing'
the butcherbird the wattlebird the chain-
saw the telephone et cetera   but
bad luck   sorry mate   not today   (peck-peck-

peck)   as though the hen had not registered
his presence   & as though neither bird had
registered her own   & then a second
male   posing & posturing just like the
first   singing the exact same song   note for

note (accuracy an imperative)
but cleverly embellished with a few
extra cadences   & then Number Two's
repertoire improved upon by Number
One   & so on & so on   for at least

an hour these two duelling boys rattled their
plumage & embroidered their tunes   all in
the hope of capturing the attentions
of the relatively silent & quite
unimpressed female   sorry   (peck-peck-peck)

🐕

what a plethora of benefits was
to be drawn from J's temporary life
on the hilltop   1—a particular
sitting place proffered not only a most
magnificent view of the city of

Melbourne but provided perspective on
all those people all those relationships
far far away down there   indeed it all
seemed like a dream   especially when lit
up at night   small   insignificant   no

threat   2—the quiet noise of evening   so
insistent so alive so innately
other to the cacophony of cars
sirens voices gadgets (far far away
down there)   3—the slowness of minutes   J

would scrutinise the hands of her watch as
though they were microscopic cells   she would
check double-check triple-check   only x
o'clock?   she actually had time to
be   & of course there were the treks with her

dog   the high heat of summer tempered by
altitude they followed meandering
paths   passed postcard scenes of Friesian cows &
still-green grass   wondered at the huge girths of
hundred-year-old manna gums   inhaled the

scent of flora & moss   &—covering
more ground than the proverbial country
mile—returned hungry & suitably tired
to The Shack   once over the trauma of
the mountain road trip Jack's hours were fully

occupied with the sights smells sounds of this
foreign but benign environment   he
didn't care for The Shack itself (so small
that the 'bedroom' was accessed by a near-
vertical ladder of sorts) but he did

enjoy its surrounds   one after-dinner
walk—during which Jack had much fun & J
almost lost her mind—the little ratter
picked up a rabbit's scent   & was gone   &
she means *gone*   calling & calling for at

least two hours   J had finally given
up   (she forgives you if you interpret
'two hours' to mean 'ten minutes'—country time
being what it is—but assures you it *was*
because she sat there   in the bush   on a

log   weeping   until the sun had long slunk
away)   again she realised   as though
for the first time   how much she loved Her Dog
who was gone   a strange thing often happens
when one finally gives up (trying to

start a stubborn car) (trying to potty-
train a stubborn toddler)   as though it is
the actual giving up—the letting
go—which is central & essential to
the resolution   thus as J sat there

in the bush   on a log   weeping   till the
sun had long slunk away   a dirt-ridden
leaf-covered exhausted dog emerged from
the darkness of the bush & leapt—without
apology—onto her already

cool resigned & very lonesome lap   she
couldn't believe it   Jack the Ratter!   Jack
had come back!   Her Dog!   her naughty naughty
self-serving rabbit-chasing dog   she hugged
him & scolded him   berated & kissed

him   held him & yelled at him all the way
back   & she never   no never   let him
off-leash in the bush again   *I am not*
the gone away   no I am not   I am
running the little thing that smells like must

chase   we have the run for the long time   that
little thing & me   until I lose the
see in the no-light   & because the thing
has the very fast   but I am never
the gone away   I have the recall for

the tree & the leaf & the rock   so I
can have the get Home again to Her &
I do   but I see she has the much sad
then   example   the wet-face & the hold
too squash   & I see she has the angry

then   example   the big rebukement &
the smack   & I see she has the happy
then   example   the cuddle-cuddle &
stroke-stroke-stroke   & indeed she has   because
I do come back to our Home   & to Her

🐕

so yes   J cried on the mountain   at a
variety of decibels   for a
variety of reasons   she listened
to sad (bad) songs & wrote bad (sad) poems
up there   she experienced examined

& acknowledged her losses up there   she
walked & sat & walked & sat & walked &
sat & wept up there   she vented the full
spectrum of emotions   & she walked   &
she sat   & she thought   & she finally

sorted things out   deals were done   a house was
bought   & J found herself (& her kids!) (&
her dog!) below the mountain   in a court
at least   with a nearby reserve at least
& a whole host of human (& doggy)

encounters to come   she had been away
& she had come back   just like little Jack
in the bush   she had survived & she had
started again   she had picked herself up
& brushed herself off   she was in one piece

moving day—another house another
start—& J was given her very own
keys to her very own place at last   she
felt good despite the daunting task ahead
relocating/unpacking/beginning

again   the new dwelling stood opposite
a winding dirt track which led into the
reserve they would soon dub Little Park   J
perceived a quietude a calmness in
the air   & believed some sort of peace may

46

be attained   she had the assistance of
both offspring on this day of days   perfect
timing in that daughter & son were due
to depart for the Top End on a two-
week sojourn with their father the very

next morning   with happy tenacity
the kids completed trip after trip from
Shack to Home in their dad's ute   transporting
load after load   up the steep driveway   up
fourteen steep steps   & finally into

the house   later that evening the three
of them sat down on boxes to bowls of
steaming soup   & then meal gone   kids gone   J
was now most definitely alone   her
spirits sank at a frightening rate as

she saw the work still to be done   apart
from the books (all forty-three cartons) there
were many other issues   kitchen &
laundry to organise   piles of clothes to
sort   planks to ratchet into beds   things to

connect   security to arrange   &
personal details—bank/insurance/et
cetera—to change   outside it threatened
to rain   inside threatened despair   & there
remained the certain little issue of

a certain Little Man   *I am not of*
the know for the now happenings   I have
the smell & see of the familiars
but never the why for the now   where is
here is the ask I have significant

need for the know   I have the smell & see
of the bed & The Ball   I have the smell
& see of Her   but she is with the what-
what look of no-speak   not the wet-face not
the laugh-face   & I am with the distinct

worry-worry at this now sphere   I do
the invitation with The Ball   but she
is with the no-thing   I do the lick of
the no-face   but she is off with the far
away   I have the try of all-thing   but

she is with the much away   the too much
away from me   & I do not have the
here of where I am or the where of where
is here   this is of the great dire & I
have not the know or the what-what to do

J sat on her new floor at half past two
in the morning   she had slept for an hour
on a sheetless mattress with a book as
her pillow & a couple of coats for
warmth   she sat there in a motionless daze

as her few friends snored after outings or
barbecues   & her kids dreamed somewhere near
Katherine Gorge   then something tapped her on
the foot   once   twice   thrice   O Jack   Our Brother
Jack (comma) Kerouac (full stop)   You are

there   As always   *You are there*   covered from
head to toe in the grime of too many
moves   too many life changes   J sat on
the floor & looked at the Little Man   she
inhaled deeply the dusty air & took

stock   Time to exhale   Time to get real   Time
to get back on track   as J began to
unpack one box after another she
heard the demons   she felt the demons   but
she would not give in she would not give in

J must have covered miles during the course
of that first day & night   trudging from room
to room   up & down stairs   from inside to
outside to inside again   &—shadowed
unfailingly by Jack—the devoted

Little Man must have covered the same ground
as her   she suspects adrenalin played
a crucial role in helping her achieve
all she did (as for Jack   well the pooch was
fuelled by love & love alone)   the pair did

not pause for food rest or diversion &—
whatever the impetus that kept them
going—their momentum did not falter
until noon the next day   by then books sat
on bookshelves   clothes hung in wardrobes   forks lay

in drawers   bathroom cupboards & linen press
were full   beds were built   comestibles hid
in both larder & fridge   electronics/
electrics all hooked up & happily
blinking   a few pictures had found their way

onto walls   boxes had been emptied &
flattened & stowed   & so let it be known
it was finally official   they had
moved in   & they had themselves a Home   *I*
am too much with the exhaustion to have

the worry-worry now   I have the big
hope for the distinct clarify soon   but
now I do the walk behind   I do not
lose the sight of Her   & I have the know
wherever she is   that is my reside

by the time J's kids returned   the new house
felt as though it had always been Home   she
was proud of how comfortable it had
so quickly become   a short leafy stroll
from the centre of town   'their' court was all

but traffic-free & the loudest sounds were
those originating from the throats of
birds or the odd distant train   daughter &
son seemed relaxed & revitalised post-
holiday &—like her—ready for this

fresh phase of life   & Jack   yes even Jack
had eventually given the paws-
up for his fourth abode   certainly it
had taken a number of rainfalls to
erase the odour of former doggy

lodgers   but it was official   even
for Jack   this here   this now   was Home   *I have*
the comprehend of the start again stay-
place   & have considered the extents of
the everything   there is the like of the

run-space & feel of safe   & the much like
of the see-through where I have the watch of
doings below   but the most like is the
smile of Her & the girl & the boy   I
am having of all happy like the king

🐕

solitary by nature   meeting the
street was not high on J's agenda   one
neighbour however was quick to extend
convivial greetings   W—a
septuagenarian of rare warmth &

wit—tackled the steep driveway & fourteen
steep steps   bottle of white wine in one hand
walking-stick in the other   to convey
a friendly hello   knock-knock   Who's there?   Hi
I'm W   Welcome to our little

court   despite the multitudinous tasks
awaiting attention (it was only
Day Four) J opened the door   escorted
W into the lounge   offered her
a glass of aforementioned wine   & sat

down   as it soon transpired this was not their
first conversation   J—healthy enough
to return to the workforce—was employed
at the nearby bookshop where W
was a regular face   as they talked it

also transpired that W was a
keen consumer of poetry (she would
prove an indispensable reader of
J's efforts in that genre for many
years to come)   the two women instantly

clicked & began to exchange numerous
books   each converting the other to a
profusion of formerly unknown or
unread works   discussions following such
literary trade-offs were frequent &

invigorating   a predilection
for certain music & films was also
shared & a system of trafficking soon
in place   respective letterboxes were
employed as pick-up/drop-off points &—in

order to herald a 'deposit'—a
windmill flower (W) or a hot
pink scarf (J) was brightly displayed in a
window   together the two attended
cinema & stage & swapped emails *en*

français   W had always been owned
by a dog   & her current pooch Kali
(aka Doggess of Destruction) will
shortly enter the story at hand   an
extraordinary friendship had begun

Kali was a six-year-old Staffordshire
cross with a voice rivalling that of Dame
Joan   she possessed the energy of a
Romanian gymnast   especially
when visitors were around   but she was

a well-behaved hound with a heart as full
as her song   after a few weeks of court
life J thought it time for Kali & Jack
to meet   it was a fine idea with
the exception of one fatal flaw   Jack

had The Ball in his jaws   knock-knock   Who's there?
It's Jack come to say hello   W
opened the door so the dogs could greet snout
to snout   but of course—dear Reader—Jack was
not the only ball-obsessed canine in

the court   upon sight Kali flew into
instinctive & immediate attack
mode   after all The Ball was in *her* house
so The Ball must be *hers*   thus she yelped &
dove at Jack   who—trapped between wall & book-

case—had no escape   despite two voices
four feet & a walking-stick the women
were unable to intercept & then
Jack lunged at the door & was out like a
shot   J later found him quivering &

wedged in the space behind her son's desk   &—
deaf to her pleas—he did not come out for
a very long time   it wasn't Kali's
fault   as Isaac Watts wrote   'Let dogs delight
to bark & bite / For God hath made them so'

I am with the fear of Kali   I want
to have the like but I am with the much
frighten   because I have the remind from
the long ago   & I carry that big
remember with me wherever the where

I am   as I have the must   & then it
is the happen all again   & I am
with the entrapment   it is the happen
again with the loud-loud & the sudden
& the scare   after the long I am out

& away with the extra fast & the
must   I stay with the hide until I have
the do of the breathing again   then I
have the squash-squash kiss & cuddle from Her
& I am with the little bit better

despite this awkward introduction   both
ownees trusted a comradely rapport
might develop between the two dogs   to
this end all four would meet in W's
front garden   dogs safe on leashes & The

Ball safe at Home   as a result of these
casual sniff-snuffle events   Kali
& Jack were gradually able to
put their differences aside   hackles
began to lower   ears began to lift

tails began to wag   & there was a whole
pack of other pooches to meet in the
court as well   each residence seemed to house
one (or two)   indeed it was Oliver
Goldsmith's poem come to life   'And in that

town a dog was found / As many dogs there
be / Both mongrel puppy whelp & hound / &
curs of low degree'   beginning at the
top end of the court (& it was not a
long court) were the Big Barkers (Alsatians)

whose names J did not know & did not want
to know   next—two doors down—pretty little
Poppy the Poodle whose thin piercing yap
sounded oddly un-dog-like   then Lil &
Lucy the Jack Russell duo   Monty

the mutt   Goldie the rarely heard/rarely
seen Golden Retriever   & then closer
to Home   Maggie   a black & white bitsa
whose name reflected her ownee's dogged
support of the Magpies (black & white) foot-

ball team   & next door to the right   Susie
the Staffy   & then next door to the left
Cromwell the King Charles Cavalier   &
finally   at the far end of the court
two fluffy white Terriers   Haggis the

Westie & Caesar the Maltese   & so
their new Home proved not only a quiet
& stable environment in which to
live & be   but a decidedly dog-
oriented world as well   Our Brother

Jack (like J   a natural isolate)
had never before been surrounded by
so many doggy sights & sounds & scents
&—although this took some getting used to—
he fast grew confident that his house was

his house   that he possessed a retreat where
he could relax & recover before
re-entering the Great Outdoors   & J
hoped a few friendships may flourish (over
the fence so to speak) to alleviate

Jack's long hours alone while she worked her own
long hours at the bookshop   *I have the much*
sense of the great many beings in this where
of here   & I have the perhaps desire
for a companionable   because she

is often of the long-long away   &
because Boss Dog is never of the true
companionable   Boss Dog is of the
much unprediction   sometimes he is of
the very tall   sometimes he is of the

small   & sometimes he is not of the here
at all   yes when I have the long apart
from Her I have the sometime wonder &
the perhaps wish of a being like me   but
then she is here   & I am of complete

🐕

patterns were swiftly established   J worked
her forty or so hours each week while Jack
did his own forty or so hours back at
Home   J's bedroom overlooked the court &
W reported Little Man as

spending much of his day observing the
goings-on below   his small face clearly
visible from W's lounge-room   both
kids were happily occupied   her son
having commenced his university

course & her daughter approaching the end
of hers   the high front balcony—favoured
on summer nights—was referred to as The
Riviera   & the back porch—complete
with plants chairs candles & hammock—fondly

christened The Place To Be   while J was no
longer in active wound-licking mode   she
was certainly uninterested in
pursuing any relationship of
a romantic order   content enough

to rub shoulders with kids & neighbour &
dog   after bookshop or between poems
she & Jack explored their purlieu   Big Park
became Saturday's regular pit-stop
where she could watch her son play tennis on

the courts abutting grasslands & creek   the
Home was often filled with voices other
than their own   in particular Wednesday
quickly transformed into 'open house' at
dinner time   this being Basketball Night (son)

& Volleyball Night (daughter) with any
number of mouths turning up for a pre-
match feed   the odd evening was spent at
an orchestral event of her daughter's
(French horn)   others simply chatting in front

of tele   however the 'no-light' (to
borrow Jack's vernacular) mostly saw
the three of them engaged in various
projects on their various computers
calling out periodically a

question a request a joke   & with Jack
punctiliously checking on each by
turn   Life Is Good?   indeed it was   these days—
however—J counted her blessings on
a consistent basis   rather than take

anything (at all) for granted   *I have*
the begin of the enjoyment of the
here   I have the begin of the okay
to breathe   because she is much of the yes-
face & I am safe   life is of the good

J speculates that nothing else could scare
her so much as that moment in the bush
when she thought Jack was gone   or the day they
were assailed by the Pit-Bull cross   but there
lay a fear in the back of her mind—as

real & as constant as her love for the
dog—that would never depart   *cars*   although
Jack was now four years old & probably
had a full decade ahead in terms of
his natural life   she took alarm that

she might lose him before time   & not in
the bush   not to a rabid cur   but to
a Car   it made sense really (which was what
afforded her fear its potency) for
dogs are struck down & killed on roads every

minute of every day   & this fact is
ever more relevant for the smaller
breeds   standing eye-height to a bumper   these
littlies—no matter how smart   no matter
how well-trained—are just not able to see

it coming   the family pooch J grew
up with eventually fell victim
to death-by-car   on page three of her work-
book (written at primary school almost
four decades ago) is the sentence 'In

a few days we are going to get a
Beagle'   with a most un-Beagle-like sketch
below (this creature resembling something
like an elongated black elephant
complete with chequered 'saddle' & long green

tongue)   the words however were true & the
Beagle shortly thereafter was 'got'   J
only qualifies the truth of this as
a number of other bulletins in
the workbook are so obviously false

(for example   'When we went to Puppa's
house his dog was dead on the roof'   apart
from the fact Puppa was not even owned
by a dog   dogs are not climbers)   indeed
J's mum had at some point added the words

'& dreams' beneath the title *News Items*
on the front cover   Caspar the Beagle
was a pedigree boasting manifold
longstanding championship genes & not
many brains   he was difficult to train

as his attention span was—to put it
politely—limited   the pooch had a
penchant for chasing motorbikes & the
postie never approached their letterbox
without a pocketful of stones   Caspar

would not Sit Lie Down Roll Over or Beg
& there was little point in washing him
as he would frolic in horse manure when
done   he didn't even appear to know
his own name   but Caspar was a happy

enough chappie & he came in handy
pulling the neighbourhood kids up the steep
hill of their street from whence they could whizz back
down on their skateboards   he was often chained
to a fence   against his predilection

to wander   but even the chain was not
always up to the task of restraining
him   there were many occasions ambling
up the driveway after school   J would spot
the chain drawn over the fence   a three-foot

leap from the roof of Caspar's kennel &—
heart in mouth—she would climb said fence & peer
down the other side   fully expecting
to see him dangling there   strangled   but he
never was   somehow—no matter how tight

the collar—the hound always managed to
wriggle out & run off unfettered to
freedom   of course lack of collar rendered
Caspar unidentifiable   &
his ownees would be subsequently forced

to ring around local council pounds &
lost dogs' homes until he was finally
found   Caspar was hit by a car three times
before the fourth & final collision
which occurred many miles from Home on one

of his unauthorised adventures   he
was only seven when he died but the
family never acquired another
dog   & so a fear was born that would not
depart   that never departed   The Car

I do not have the like for being inside
the noise-with-the-fast   no not at all   but
I do not have the like for being outside
the noise-with-the-fast too   when we are of
the perambulate on the next to the

many   loud-loud-loud   & the wind & the
rush of the smoke that stops the breathe   I have
the petrify then   because I know   if
one happens near   if one happens close   it
will conveyance me somewhere that is not

my Home   & it will compel my away
& it will be much more than the cut of
the paw & the-man-with-the-hurt   & I
will lose the happy exist with Her &
the anymore for the ever again

62

Jack's relationship to J was one of
elemental connectivity   as
hydrogen bonds with oxygen so he
did with her   & he would rather lose his
life than this bond   his existence was lived

fundamentally in relation to
hers   his being would be meaningless without
her   she was nothing less than his *raison
d'être*   his alpha & omega   his
everything   his all   Jack was not just close

to J but yoked to her   canine heart to
human heart   even until death   thus Jack's
essence could not be seen as inert   his
devotion had created of them both
a new & animate compound   Jack's high-

level response to all J's emotions
& expressions & behaviour was a
conduit   flawlessly constructed &
maintained   active or reactive (although
rarely proactive) Jack could not be called

passive   he never rested   if indeed
he did sleep it was always with one eye
open & one ear up   his only true
slumber occurred when J herself slept   &
still he was alert to the slightest move

she made   Jack was a spirit embodied
—pure energy in a physical form—
dynamic   kinetic   & utterly
charged   an unerring friend he was also
an absolute mathematical constant

J understood this was the case   & it
concerned her   it was for this reason she
preferred not to go away more often
or for longer than she must   she would have
liked to travel Australia   she would

have liked to apply for Australia
Council residencies in Paris or
Rome   she would have liked a remote island
Home for a month   but when she returned from
a necessary trip of even a

few days' duration   Jack's eyes & coat had
visibly dulled   he seemed haggard   faded
less *there*   J knew a lengthy absence would
see him fold up & die   she recalled the
plucky Skye Terrier of *Greyfriar's*

Bobby who kept vigil for fourteen years
atop his deceased master's grave in the
1850s   & the bullocky's dog
who faithfully guarded his dead ownee's
tuckerbox until he too expired 'five

miles from Gundagai'   she did not suppose
Jack was possessed by blind faith   no   Jack was
not a believer   but a thinker   a
true intellectual   Jack would ask too
many questions without any answers

Jack would pose arithmetical problems
with no solutions   Jack would pine   Jack would
eventually concede she was not
coming back   & die   *another thing I*
do not have the like for is the going

away   & it happens very much   as
soon as she does the pull down of the go-
box I have the know   & my tail has the
fall   she puts in the go-box thing by thing
& I have the know   she is performing

the go-away   it has no matter if
it is for the singular no-light or
the many no-light it is the same   go-
go-gone   & I am of the disquiet
& the discomfit for the disappear

Jack preferred order over chaos   the
predictable over surprise   being to
coming or going   ever alert for
the signs—an open suitcase   a spray of
perfume   the shopping list moving from bench

to bag   even the rattle of keys—his
anxiety was instantly plain   Jack
did not like to let J out of sight   just
as when a pup he shadowed her every
step   followed her from room to room   sat when

she sat   stood when she stood   like a spider
at the hub of its web   each strand of his
environment was trip-wired to her   &
the slightest inhalation sent ripples
of information along these threads   back

to his sensory centre   if the dog
allowed himself a short break of duty
it was only when J was involved in
an essentially familiar task
like cooking or taking a shower   still

he would poke his tiny head around the
corner from time to time   just to check   just
to make sure   he needed to know she was
not about to drive away or walk off
& then vanish   into a hospital

a shopping centre   a Venus Bay   this
obsessive state of affairs once rankled
J   but she no longer resisted the
constant escorting   the compulsive stare
or the unceasing computations   Our

Brother Jack (comma) Kerouac (full stop)
was who he was—the dogged depressive/
the phobic fanatic/the calculus
mind with a Russian soul—& despite it
all   or because of it all   she loved him

it was the staring that J found the most
disconcerting in the early days   while
Jack used his full arsenal of senses
he was particularly vigilant
when it came to the visual front   that

said—dear Reader—he reserved different
'stares' for different situations   when
J was at the computer (often for hours at a time)   the
Little Man would hunker down near (or on)
her feet & establish a good line of

military-standard sight   from there he
could observe as she typed/stopped/peered out the
window/checked a reference book/resumed
typing/stopped/thought/gazed at the screen/returned
to typing again   sometimes J paused to

ponder for an extended period
which appeared to bother the dog   clearly
he preferred the arrhythmic music of
computer keying to the unnerving
sounds of silence   Jack's computer-stare was

characterised by much head-nodding as
he struggled to stay awake   during a
particularly lengthy session   he
would finally register a polite
but decidedly firm request to be

removed from floor to lap   to achieve this
Jack issued a constant small & almost-
human *ooh* until J acquiesced   now
it is no simple task to type behind/
above/around the body of a dog

but she did   as to Jack's tele-stare   have
you ever attempted to lose yourself
in an absorbing crime or intricate
plot while being beheld?   Jack would stand before
the couch   staring-at-J-staring-at-the-

screen   until the machine was at last switched
OFF   J had played both flute & piano
for many years & had recently bought
a cello   Jack's cello-stare was expressed
modo religioso   no sooner

had she placed music on music-stand   he
knew   before she lifted tuning fork or
rosin or bow   he knew   as poorly as
J played   the cello itself seemed to have
an ecstatic effect on Jack   sitting

in what could only be classed as canine
lotus position he appeared to *go
inward*—to meditate so to speak—in
response to the physical vibrations
of horsehair reverberating upon

catgut over a hollow body of
rosewood & blonded spruce   his eyes remained
open but—like a Tibetan Buddhist—
only just   the most disturbing of all
was Jack's please-don't-leave-me-stare   this one had

no ready reply   no remedy   when
J had to go away   she had to go
away   &—as explained above—she did
so only when necessary   as soon
as the process of leaving began   Jack's

eyes became simply un-look-back-into-
able   from the moment of picking up
purse/bag/keys/case the situation was
dire beyond dire   the woman could not look
the dog in the eye   & the dog *would not*

look back anyway   If I could I would!
she enthusiastically tried to
convey   (Silence)   If you knew where I was
going you would not want to come!   (Silence)
the guilt was almost intolerable

but—for life to continue—food must be
bought   bills must be paid   & certain trips must
be made   *non   nein   nyet*   NO!   o lordy   what
to do?   You need to get a life! she would
cry   as the dog looked the opposite way

🐕

the more irritating aspects of Jack's
unwavering devotion aside   J
concedes that without his devotion she
may not be here today   she does not mean
in the emotional sense (though it is

true   the Little Man indeed 'saved' her from
herself a couple of times)   but in the
very real very practical sense   once
she left a pot on the stove & forgot
& went to bed   *I have the sniff of the*

wrong-wrong & I am taken by the much
scare   I must do the duty & give Her
the let-know with the fast   but she is with
dream-dream & has not the pricking up of
ears   I perform the run around with the

again & again until she has the
wake   & does the go to fix   I myself
do the hide until the squealer cease &
she makes the all okay   & after the
long we return to the sleep-place   & I

have done the significant of duty
& I have not let Her away of my
sight   but I cannot do the dream-dream for
the remain of the no-light   no Brave Boy
she kept saying   *Brave Boy Brave Boy Brave Boy*

as both daughter & son began to spend
less time at Home & more time involved with
activities & friends & The World   J
began to brood on the numerous hours
Jack must endure alone   she could not help

but wonder if a 'sister' or 'brother'
might be a thought   but her solutions to
problems were so often misplaced   could she
afford the extra expense   the extra
responsibility   the extra love

& what would Little Man think?   would he feel
comforted or displaced?   befriended or
abandoned?   considered or neglected?
& thus she mused—for a number of months—
heeding the old Buddhist adage   'Never

make a decision when the path is un-
clear'   already possessing a certain
melancholia   it was Jack's descent
into what seemed true doggy depression
that eventually forced her hand   yes—

for better or worse—they would invite a
second pooch to join their little clan   this
time there was no research as such   pet shop
pooches are often put to sleep at the
age of five months (people generally

desiring a 'puppy' as opposed to
a 'dog') & so J started to scour these
outlets rather than *The Trading Post* or
internet   she wanted to save a dog
doomed   however—Christmas only a week

behind—finding a dog was easier
said than done   J visited poochless pet
shop after poochless pet shop   travelling
further & further afield   until she
finally located a pokey place

with no fewer than *thirteen* contenders
all in the one cramped cage   J responded
immediately to one female in
particular   dusky fawn   sedate &
withdrawn as Jack had been at that age   but

'that age' was only twelve weeks & she knew
this sweetie-pie would procure an ownee
with ease   so J requested another
female—this one two days short of five months
(& thus two days short of eternal sleep)—

to be removed from the cage for a meet
& greet   the pup in question was black with
white points & face & very (yes *very*)
animated   careening around the
place   skidding across corners & slipping

into things   bumping over fish tanks &
pamphlet stands   jumping up at J   yipping
loudly & in no uncertain terms   *thank*
you for letting me adopt you! yip! i
love you already! yip! get me outta

here!   well okay   choice made   by canine not
human design   although that minor fact
did not appear of import to either
party   J did feel a grinding regret
however   driving off in the knowledge

the new family member had left a
true blood brother back there in the cage   who
had only a couple of days before
his own scheduled departure to doggy
heaven   but this was something she could not

afford to dwell on   & she always hoped
that he did indeed find an earthly Home
in time   *i knew it! i knew it! i knew*
she was gonna pick me as soon as she
got in the door even tho she looked at

pookie girl first i knew she'd pick me cos
i'm mollie! & i'm the one for her! &
now i'm outta the cage where everyone
keeps standing on me & yapping at me
& peeing in my face yip yip hooray!

🐕

it was with trepidation that J drove
Evil Mollie Flanders—from wherever
had that name emerged?—Home   what would Little
Man's reaction be?   her daughter's?   her son's?
while J had considered a second dog

for some time   she had not actually
deliberated with anyone   would
it succeed or would it fail?   was she the
cleverest or stupidest person you
have ever met?   in either case it was

an inviolable commitment   she
had been acquired by another Dog   this
was no flippant social experiment
or quirky *Brady Bunch* episode   no
this was real   & it simply had to work

🐕

enter Mollie!   life-loving bling-wearing
Heinz 57   fearless streetwise punk-
of-a-pup   couch-leaping limb-draping eye-
blinking mutt   princess panda-face   circus-
act whirling on black & white pins   ditzy

queen of the 5pm *yip!*   their 'special'
girl with the Joker grin   their autistic
asthmatic delinquent addition   their
distraction   their despair   their gorgeous &
only Moll   Mollie's name?   well it must be

assumed that Daniel Defoe's novel *Moll
Flanders* was subliminally at work
in the background here   but the 'Evil'?   now
Mollie was most certainly not *evil*
in the true sense of the word   & one can

only surmise that the seemingly more
negative of her 'virtues'—wilfulness/
stubbornness/mischievousness/aberrant
scheming/individualism/a
thorough & firm independence—somehow

at some early juncture   gave rise to the
appellative prefix so readily
embraced   Evil Mollie Flanders   hmm   not
quite the splendid nomenclature granted
to Our Brother Jack (comma) Kerouac

(full stop)   but a name (what's in a name?) all
the same   & so again   enter Miss Moll-
ie!   the moment the new pup waltzed—that is
sped/slid/darted/dove—into the house   it
was already hers   Mollie's expletives

(which she must have learned in The Pet Shop) were
many & varied & positively
'yippy'   yes   she b%@@$# loved this place   yes
this was her b%@@$# Home   & yes she was
here to b%@@$# well stay   & this time the

ownee in question had thankfully thought
just a little ahead   thus there was a
special bed   a special bowl   some special
toys et cetera   but such things seemed—quite
literally—immaterial to

Mollie   Mollie had a Home   & a Home
was all the new daughter of the estate
had desired   Mollie was out of her cage
Mollie was Free   it was all that mattered
Freedom   how often do we hear that   as

humans?   freedom as *the* most desired thing
above all else   it was most certainly
cause to think   *i am so happy! but i*
miss my bro i am so happy! yip! but
i miss my bro i hope he is ok

as a matter of course Evil Mollie
Flanders gave Jack a passing sniff   the new
pooch was unconcerned that Home may be of
the house-sharing variety   after
all   she had spent her first few paltry months

on this earth living just so   amongst an
array of similarly impounded
pedigrees   mongrels   curs   &—for his part—
Jack was similarly unconcerned   he
had witnessed almost as many canines

pass through his own abode   & had (somewhat)
enjoyed these experiences   so   no
love lost   for now   in fact Jack seemed to like
Mollie at first   & a lot   how can this
be properly put?   Mollie was new   she

was a diversion   & as someone new
she was—in her unique way—someone who
was a sensual & feminine being
who was simply *there*   certainly Jack had
'fallen in love' before—Shem (ownee K)

& Xena (ownee Y)—but   & this was
an enormous BUT   these girls had possessed
their own residences to which they would
always return   not so it would seem with
Evil Mollie Flanders   no   it would seem

Mollie was here to stay   hmm   to begin
with the Little Man was dapper   even
enchanting so to speak   however   as
it dawned on him that the intruder was
not about to Go Away it also

occurred to him that this may not be the
perfect in-house relationship he was
gunning for   & so let the fun begin
I do not have the like   I do not have
the like   no   I do not have the like of

her   Mollie is of the nice-nice I have
the must confess   but I do not have the
like of her in the being of here   this here
is of the particular mine & my
comprehend is of the much challenge   there

has happened not one not two but three no-
lights & she is still of the here   the my
of here   she is doing the yip all round
the darkness house   & I am having the
no-sleep   & I am having the get up

with Her to do the attend & shoosh of
Mollie   & I am having the no-like
at all   this here is of the very mine
the much of mine   & I do not have the
like   I do not   I do not   I do not

🐕

as mentioned above   J had indulged in
no academic research where Mollie's
'breed' was concerned   she had simply wanted
a pal to befriend & occupy the
Little Man   she had not even cared if

this new pooch was Non-Allergenic or
what   in reality she had never
actually considered herself as
allergic to canines   just cats   indeed
she reflected on her decidedly

dogged inquiry into dogs as a
potential cause for anaphylaxis
as bordering on paranoid   (& yes
she had been defeated by illness at
the time)   Mollie's roots were a delightful

& unqualified mix   the pup was a
true world citizen   her papers—such as
they were—stated one quarter Pug (thus the
big eyes   the beautiful double-layered
eyelashes)   one quarter Maltese (the two-

fingers' width black nose)   one quarter King Charles
Cavalier (the drop ears   the piebald
colouring)   & one quarter 'some kind of
Terrier')   as Mollie matured & J
became more familiar with the new

dog's character   it was the 'some kind of
Terrier' element that never quite
added up   Mollie was no Terrier
in the sense that Jack most definitely
was   she was no ratter   she displayed no

interest at all in The Ball   no   she
was much more consumed by 'rounding up' both
ownee & Jack   embarking on a walk
Mollie—despite leash—would nose at the back
of J's legs   determinedly herding

said legs toward Little Park   unleashed she
would trot or race against Jack   all the while
firmly adhered to his flank   conducting
direction from her dominant droving
position   in addition   Moll's spatial

intelligence was highly developed
for such a young thing   while Jack (so canny
& quick-witted in so many ways) was
prone to entanglement with poles & trees
when on-leash   Mollie was able to dis-

entangle herself with ease   indeed she
seemed to respond intuitively to
verbal commands   Round you go!   *Round* you go!
which fell deaf on Jack's otherwise astute
ears   yet Moll exhibited little or

no reaction to Jack's favourite (ball-
related) directive   Go Get It!   it
was this kind of behaviour which led J
to believe that 'some kind of Terrier'
was some kind of misprint for 'some kind of

sheepdog'   no matter   Mollie was who she
was   (& yes   Jack   she was here to stay)   *i*
love being here i love being here i love being
here with her & jack & the boy & the
girl i just love everything everywhere

cos this is the life! there's so much to smell
& see & explore & do & i love
yipping at people & racing cross the
road & chasing jackie round the table
& chucking the cushions off the couch &

chewing the books & sit! & stay! & come
on then! i love all of it all the time
& i love it at night cos i get so
tired & i just wanna curl up next to
my jackie & her & sleep for a bit

daily life with Evil Mollie Flanders
was as mixed as the new dog's pedigree
in that Mollie provided delight &
despair in equal measure   the household
(Jack included) seemed caught on some kind of

pendulum   swinging constantly between
reprimand & praise   ire & affection
laughter & teary frustration   on the
up side   Mollie was an infectiously
light-hearted pup   & her unquestioning

& unrelenting enthusiasm
for life in general created an
instantly positive hit for any
within her vicinity   Moll embraced
the world with all four 'arms'   indeed   even

at rest—on the floor   or preferably
astride the back of a couch—her legs were
splayed outward as though she were a rug made
from some nineteenth-century safari
hunter's prize   in contrast to Little Man

the Little Girl was disarmingly self-
sufficient   she would wander around house
& yard wholly immersed in her inner
notions & explorations   & even
invented her own entertainment   one

game involved poking a particular
purple rabbit through the slats of the lounge-
room coffee table   then retrieving it
(often with serious difficulty
& a remarkably sustained effort)

with a paw   this could keep her occupied
for an hour or more   Mollie also liked
upending her bed to conceal a toy
& then righting the bed &—*voilà!*—there
was the toy! (yes   again & again &

again)   yet another game entailed one
of her many 'babies'   she would sit it
up & lie in front like a sphinx   gazing
into said baby's eyes   before gently
returning it to the miniature house

which was used to store doggy toys   (note   each
& every one of such 'babies' had been
found by Mollie in Little Park   these were
obviously soft toys fallen from a
stroller or pram   & the dog would bring them

Home   held ever so tenderly in jaw
to add to her collection   favourites
included a cross-eyed orange penguin
& a disturbingly smiley fork-tailed
devil)   the above illustrates to some

extent Moll's deep maternal instincts   once
again this idiosyncrasy found
no correspondence within Jack   who would
first remove the eyes of a soft toy (so
quickly one may think he was spooked) before

systematically disembowelling
it   & then destroying the poor 'baby'
altogether   however—& J does
not find this fact insignificant—Jack
never   *ever*   harmed any of Mollie's

designated toys   yes Mollie truly
loved her babies   & was also partial
to mothering (or endeavouring to
mother) actual infants—canine or
otherwise—licking faces   keeping watch

staying as close as the situation
permitted   further   whenever J found
herself in a weepy moment   Jack would
disappear—unnerved/disoriented
by any display of grief—while Mollie

on the other hand   would not desert J's
side   tonguing her tears   rhythmically tapping
her cheek   her shoulder   her ankle with a
reassuring paw   & Jack somehow seemed
to respect all of this   perhaps—even

in the doggy world—there is Men's Business
& there is Women's Business   again—in
fundamental contradiction to Jack—
Mollie possessed an utter disregard
for routine   for her anything went (as

long as she did too)   be it day or night
if something was happening   Mollie would
be found at its epicentre   the dog
was fearless (no Personal Phobia
List here) & would try whatever   be it

belly-flopping into puddles   wrestling
pillows or toys in cetacean-like death-
rolls   attempting to fly after galah
or cockatoo   or expelling her own
reflection from the creek   the Little Girl

would eat anything as well   from birdseed
to tofu to newspaper to snails   her
strong constitution a never-ending
scientific marvel   Mollie enjoyed
playing dress-ups &—apart from 'babies'—

would often discover a scrap of foil
or tinsel or fabric in Little Park
& tote it Home   not content until her
find was fastened onto neck like a string
of pearls *haute couture*   she would spin around

& around & around on skinny hind
legs in delight   indeed a travelling
carnival crossed J's mind more than once   which
brings us to the down side of things   Mollie
was naughty   a true rascalette   & [*no*

i'm not!] contrary   she liked to provoke
especially when it came to Jack   her
selected sport was stalking   during a
walk Mollie would run ahead   turn back to
face the Little Man   lie flat on the ground

(convinced such a position rendered her
completely invisible) & Wait   as
Jack tentatively approached—knowing full
well what lay in store   & knowing also
he must pass Moll (the Troll) in order to

get Home himself—Mollie would suddenly
lunge   head down   barrelling toward him as
though he were the red rag & she were the
bull   bowling him quite off his feet   Jack was
then forced to dust himself off like a drunk

from a brawl   & pretend that nothing had
happened at all   once he had physically
& psychologically recovered (for
the Alpha Male had been truly shamed) Moll
would saunter off ahead   swinging her hips

like a Sumo   Jack never got his head
around Mollie's idea of such a
grand game   which only worked to further her
evident relish in bedevilling
him   (Our Brother Jack was never amused)

*Mollie is with the distinct penchant for
the run-run at me   & I am not of
the like   I have the only to go back
to the stay-place with Her   but Mollie is
of the much obstacle & makes of the*

*big un-do   I have the possess of the
distinguish but Mollie is of the no-
see   & I am with the difficult to
find the what-what of my feet again &
to have the sustain of a being like me*

hee hee i love this game i love this game
cos jackie boy thinks he's sooo smart with all
the big words & stuff & he thinks he's the
master cos he's older but mollie is
bigger! yip! mollie rules! & anyhoo

he needs to know about fun & i so
love his face when he gets back up like he
never had his nose in the dirt he looks
so peed off & i'm so full of laughing
yip! jackie boy's the boy for me ok!

Evil Mollie proving a challenging
customer when it came to 'training' J
almost gave up several times   whilst she
understood the task may be trickier
than it had been with Jack—Mollie's pet shop

origins   where eating/sleeping/playing/
peeing all occur in one spot   & Jack
from a family environment   with
routines in place & actual mother
as living breathing example—she did

not dream it would ever be this hard   the
dog simply resisted discipline in
every imaginable way   on top
of it all the vet pronounced Little Girl
autistic   & directed J to the

book *Animals in Translation* for a
convincing argument re autism
in dogs   *what?* well okay   Moll did seem to
inhabit her own private world   rarely
meeting eyes with anyone other than

her babies   &—as affectionate &
happy as she was—existed on a
completely separate plane   but this was
too much   autistic?   the human/canine
communication lines may have appeared

somewhat limited with Mollie   but hey
in comparison to the long complex
'conversations' that could be shared with Jack
anyone could be deemed autistic   &
anyway Good Golly Miss Mollie she

was *loved*   after much trouble & fuss   house-
training was achieved   what a relief to
say the least   at last the new pooch seemed to
comprehend that certain activities
take place inside the Home   & others out

in the yard   this was—perhaps—one small step
for dogkind   but a giant leap for young
Mollie   & the achievement had not been
without drama   indeed one friend staying
a few days had insisted on taking

it upon himself to mend Moll of her
unruly ways   this by application
of the Iron Rod Principle   although
Mollie responded reasonably well
to his tactics   the dog obviously

harboured more than a little resentment
& one night—in full view of all humans
present—she jumped up & crouched on the couch
&   looking each in the eye   released a
long stream of Don't Tell Me What To Do pee

*i'm not scared of nothing no nothing! not
like jackie boy no! i'm not scared of cars
or trains or kids or thunder or nothing
at all not even that mister bossy
boots who leads her round half the time no not*

*even that stupid old dog! he's just a
wimp anyhoo cos when i lick off her
tears & hug her neck he gets smaller &
smaller right there in front of me till he's
just teeny weeny like the most teeny*

*weeny wimp & sometimes i can even
make him go all the way away like i'm
magic & that's mollie! i'm bigger &
stronger cos i'm here & i'm mollie &
mollie's not scared of nothing ok yip!*

when J left for work each morning   there were
now two mournful little faces pressed to
her bedroom window   & her return each
evening was heralded by two (one
yapping) (one yipping) overjoyed dogs   J

felt much happier in the knowledge that
Jack had a 'companionable'   although
the two dogs did not always see eye to
eye   & there did occur the odd in-house
tiff   at least he was not alone   within

a matter of weeks   Evil Mollie had
become part & parcel of the household
however—despite the swiftness with which
she had exceeded Little Man in both
body weight & height—Jack had wasted no

time establishing himself as the no-
questions-asked Alpha Male   & Mollie could
not have cared less   did not blink a double-
layered eyelash   *yip! i let jackie boy*
think he's the ruler cos he's gotta think

that he is & act like he is while all
the time i know i'm mollie & i'm the
real ruler cos i'm bigger than him &
i know wot to do & i do it &
i get jackie boy when he least expects!

Life Was Good   so why did depression creep
in again?   J tried to reason with it
but depression is not rational   &
it does whatever it pleases   J had
never been robust   & her old friend Dread

waited in the wings like a fan for an
autograph   waited until the curtain
dropped & then tenderly took her by the
hand & removed her from the stage   J did
not know why   but there it was   as the months

tip-toed by she receded further &
further into herself   her need for food
& sleep diminished   she was visited
daily by Dread   &—after almost five
years of stability—she found herself

poised for a direct head-on collision
with life   *I am having the deep despair*
that Boss Dog is of the much huge size in
these days   Boss Dog is up at the very
rooftop high & I have the great fear for

the not-again   with Her doing the go-
around in the no-light   I have the more
endeavour to bring her The Ball & the
happy   but she is not having the see
of me   & Boss Dog has the keep of Her

on the strict pull-lead   I am of the full
alarm she will do the big go away
again   & I must not be letting Her
out from my eyes   it is the much duty
of me   the much significant duty

alright ok even mollie is scared
even mollie is scared by old mister
bossy boots even tho mollie is big
yes i'm big! but boss boots is bigger &
even i am scared of that dog today

so   ignoring unwieldy detail—dear
Reader—the collision occurred & it
was spectacular   more hospital more
hopelessness & another job lost   this
time J had not one canine physician

but two   without Little Man & Mollie
her convalescence would have been slower
& so much more taxing   this she knew as
fact   J's daughter was living in a mud
hut in Africa   & her son was on

scholarship in America   &—while
she was relieved they had been spared the full
force of her illness—she had certainly
missed their love & support   as a result
the part played by the pooches was clearly

crucial   it was an irony that a
few months after Mollie joined their clan as
a 'companionable' for the Little
Man   J found herself with unlimited
time at Home   however she never (or

perhaps let us say *rarely*) regretted
the Little Girl's arrival   the two dogs
had swiftly developed a workable
drill   with Jack awarded Top Dog rights   &
Moll content in the subservient (though

not for a moment *second-class*) role   as
a result of J's new situation
walks & playtime became more frequent   &—
apart from the odd piece of panic—these
were increasingly Dread-free times   their house

stood on a steep block   & a narrow up-
hill path punctuated by a hairpin
left turn provided access to the high
backyard   prior to Mollie's rambunctious
rock-rollicking ready-for-anything

entry   the Little Man had designed a
strategy by which he could roll The Ball
down the path   right to the end   without it
spilling off the edge   this meant somehow 'pre-
programming' said Ball to navigate the

path's dog-leg curve   no one could work out how
Jack achieved this   the uncanny feat was
filmed & scrutinised   still—apart from his
drawn out (& utterly theatrical)
precision in placing The Ball at the

top of the path before giving it a
skilful nudge of the nose—Jack's actual
methodology remained a riddle
& try as they might   none of the humans
could imitate (let alone rival) the

dog's peculiar triumph   *I am of*
the much concentrate with The Ball   because
of the very logistical & the
exact   I am having to do the think
like a ball   & when I have the think like

a ball I have the know to make it go
to the wherever I desire   & The
Ball is doing the behave of me   this
is of my great accomplish   & it is
of the very particular of me

o yes   while Moll was undeniably
Queen of Fun   Jack was undisputed King
of The Ball   his love affair with The Ball
however was about to take a life-
altering & painful turn   one morning

while in the backyard tossing The Ball to
Jack (Mollie around   no particular
purpose in mind) J threw the ball up once
again   it was a short lob & not high
but when the Little Man leapt for the catch

he landed   & just stood there   not moving
with one hind leg hanging at a strange &
sickening angle   J could not digest
what had happened   a broken leg?   no! not
possible!   ball tossing in the yard was

severely limited by the small space
itself   certainly nothing compared to
the long & miraculous throws that The
Chucker allowed in Big Park   but there he
was   just standing   unable to take a

step   Ball still in jowls   fright in his eyes   &
a sinking feeling in J   leaving Moll
to fend for herself   J gingerly picked
up Our Brother Jack   grabbed her bag   lay the
dog in the back of the car & drove off

to their lovely new vet   *wot's going on?*
wot about me? i wanna go too this
isn't fair cos i'm big & i'm mollie
& mollie is part of everything &
i should be going off with jackie boy

& her & not left on my lonesome in
the big scary house like nobody cares
& wot if boss boots comes & bites off my
head & wot if i die or something yip!
wot then? wot's happening? i wanna go too

🐕

J did not know if the news was good or
bad   no   Jack had not broken his leg   but
ruptured his cruciate ligament (known
in Aussie Rules as footballer's knee) &
this was an injury all sportspeople

feared   for it is not possible for the
ligament to reattach itself to
the patella   no matter what treatment
provided   it must be manually
stitched back in place   thus requiring (very

expensive) surgery   in order to
adequately & permanently hold
the torn connective tissue to kneecap
a suture of not insignificant
gauge is employed   as such—from the moment

the bandage was removed—the suture in
Jack's leg could always be felt as a sharp
protuberance just beneath the surface
of the skin   it was obviously a
source of constant discomfort   years on he

still sat with the leg splayed on an angle
still ran with a strange lopsided gait   &—
every so often—he still worried at
the spot in question   endeavouring to
lick the irritation away   tossing

The Ball necessarily became a
more subdued activity following
this event   The Chucker was retired to
a cupboard in the laundry   & Little
Man's life inextricably changed that day

I am of the distinct knowledge of some
bad happening then   I am doing the
motionless & not having the run back
to Her   I am doing the stand with the
what-what feel & all of the everything

change   we go in the noise-with-the-fast but
we are of the different direction
& I have the much relief   because I
do not have the like for the man-with-the-
hurt & I am wishing for not to go

there   I am wishing for the new lady-
with-the-care & that is where we have the
thankful arrive   & I am wishing she
will do the repair of me   & I am
with the very much sleepy dream-dream then

caring for Little Man post-surgery
& during convalescence enabled
J to heal more quickly herself   & Moll
as Number One Physician for them both
excelled at her new & unexpected

role   by the time Jack was properly back
on his feet   the relationship between
the two dogs had subtly altered   Mollie
appeared slightly less distracted   slightly
more focussed   & Little Man was slightly

more tolerant of Mollie's day to day
presence   not only did the Top Dog seem
to have accepted the younger pooch's
various idiosyncrasies   he
seemed to have discovered advanced methods

of dealing with them   for instance   when Moll
now did the 'run-run' at him   Jack—in an
attempt to protect his leg—simply side-
stepped her barrelling charge at the very
last moment   & when Moll stole his Ball or

bone   he just sat like a small sad boy whose
tower of blocks had been knocked over (yet
again) & looked at J until she was
alerted to the situation   &
could resolve it on his behalf   it was

clear   Jack was no longer willing to get
too physical in terms of defending
himself or his rights   he was aware of
his new limitations   but he was not
merely becoming more forbearing of

Evil Mollie   he was developing
a definite affection   when the two-
some were not squabbling like seagulls they were
in distinct cahoots   off-leash in Little
Park they would suddenly take off! at a

pace   Moll (naturally) ahead   glancing
back at Jack (remarkably not too far
behind)   in order to ascertain he
was up for The Hoot   & The Hoot was as
follows   sprinting behind the long line of

fences   the rascally duo would set
the backyard dogs a-barking—one by one—
until the entire area was a
chorusing canine cacophony   ring-
leader Mollie would then give Jack a quick

wink   as though to say Good Job!   & the two
mosey off   smirking like larrikins   to
return to the mandatory task of
sniffing & snuffling   which brings us to a
matter of the gravest importance   *pee*

in this 'business' Jack & Mollie possessed
precise & contrasting styles   perhaps as
a result of Jack's lessons coming from
mother (no father present) his approach
was—now how can this be expressed?—slightly

ladylike   thus he affected a sort
of self-conscious semi-squat by which he
himself seemed rather unconvinced   when in
a manlier mood Jack did lift a leg
but nine times out of ten it was the wrong

leg   & the (unintended) target his
opposite hind limb   on the other hand
there was Evil Moll   & the theatrics
here were nothing short of profound   slowly
lowering herself into a deep &

supplicatory bow   she rivalled a
medieval courtier on full bended
knee   feathered cap sweeping across her heart
before ceremoniously gracing
the land   as for the 'other business' the

situation was somewhat reversed   with
negligible Shakespearean flair (&
no shame whatsoever) Evil Mollie
Flanders would deposit her offering
whenever/wherever   while Jack preferred

to believe the conceit his privacy
was intact   picking his way through bracken
& grass until he considered himself
The Invisible Dog   the Little Man
would then assume a kind of Thumper stance

(*à la Bambi*) & methodically
tap one hind foot on the ground through to the
task's ultimate completion   to return
to the subject of peeing—if indeed
you are still with us dear Reader—it was

not merely *modus operandi* which
differentiated one dog from the
other   it was the location of the
event itself   Mollie liked to leave her
mark on anything different or out

of place in her immediate world   to
this end she would genuflect upon a
fallen twig/discarded newspaper/a
plastic bag or bottle/anything that
should not be where it was   Jack—however—

liked to pee on   *pee*   & preferably
Mollie's pee   walks were thus annoyingly
protracted affairs   Miss Mollie barging
ahead   busily branding various
pieces of wrongly placed detritus   &

Jackie to the rear   just as busily
overriding the statements she had so
histrionically made   by the end of
any given walk   Moll always had more
to offer—so to speak—while the Little

Man laboured to fabricate that final
priceless drop   signifying not only
I Woz Ere   but *I Woz Ere LAST!*   o the
drama   o the passion   o the precious
exquisite solemnity of it all

that shouldn't be there & that shouldn't be
there & mollie knows! & mollie loves to
fix things up for her & jackie boy &
everyone everywhere & i know wot
to do when i see the things & the stuff

wot shouldn't be there i do a pee! yip!
& if mister bossy boots went to sleep
right in front of me i would pee on his
head yes i promise i would! cos mollie
knows how to make all the bad things right yip!

🐕

scatology aside   walks were—of course—
fundamentally vital events   there
they went   Mollie tail up   Jack tail (part way)
up   this constituent of the canine
anatomy indicative of their

contrasting inner selves   in terms of flags
Moll's fully raised ensign illustrated
her unbounding enthusiasm for
life—her essential *wot's next?* attitude—
while Jack's half-mast display belied a more

cautious outlook on the world   in terms of
the proverbial glass   Mollie's was filled
to the brim   while the Little Man's was not
semi-full   but semi-empty   yes   Jack
was a pessimist   right down to the bone

🐕

on their extendable-retractable
leashes (without question another
of mankind's most inspired inventions) both
dogs were able to supplement the need
for exercise with the aspiration

to explore   assess   & reassess their
world/s   while she often felt as though she were
fishing for marlin—her arms a constant
juggle of direction/s   tangle/s   length/s—J
was able to maintain a semblance of

forward progress as the pooches circled
& pulled   this way & that   on-leash outings
were not so much walks as a dance   Mollie's
fast affection for her family was
expressed at such times in a beautiful

& unique manner   like the newly born
elephant clasped to mother's tail via
trunk   Moll curled tail around leash   preserving
physical connection with J   without
interrupting the all-important sniff-

snuffle routine   & when Jack's leash crossed or
brushed against her own   she instinctively
curled tail around that as well   in this way
Mollie was the glue in the mix   keeping
everyone secure   in touch   & affixed

J's love for Evil Mollie was also
deepening   where some saw nothing more than
a somewhat amusing nuisance   J saw
genuine beauty   by the ripe old age
of two   Mollie's appearance had matured

alongside her nature   what had begun
as a simple white collar was now a
true Elizabethan Pierrot-style
ruff   longer than the rest of her coat   &
sticking up like a wiry mane   the white

hairs on her face—similarly wiry
& quite awry—lent Moll a cute punkish
quality   most suited to her roguish
temperament   her shiny black button
nose resembled that of an old-fashioned

teddy-bear   & the black hairs surrounding
her enormous black eyes gave rise to the
nickname Princess Panda-Face   while her fore
legs remained lankier than her hind legs
the rest of her had—more or less—evened

out   & she no longer seemed a gibbon
straddling a branch when she slept across the
back of the couch   but a luxurious
lady at rest   even Mollie's bubble-
gum-coloured tongue did not detract from her

predominantly patrician air   while
Jack was a sniffer   Evil Moll was most
definitely a licker & her tongue
was in constant use   protruding ever
so slightly   this pretty pink appendage

gave the impression of a lightly lip-
sticked mouth   carefully painted before it
received its first paramour's kiss of the
evening   on the other hand   Mollie's
behaviour belied her sweet innocent

looks   & continued to preclude her from
full Lady status   to put it mildly
the dog had character   was happy-go-
lucky   a free spirit   to put it more
bluntly   she was wild   well   okay   perhaps

not *completely*   J's persistent efforts
to guide Moll along the o-so-crooked
road of obedience & self-control
had partially proven successful   for
example   the dog had finally learned

to Wait! as the front door opened   rather
than hurtling between J's legs & then down
the stairs & scooting full-speed over the
road   this scenario forewarning a
certain & imminent death-by-car   she

had grasped the terms Sit! & Get Down!   had learned
Good Dog! Come On! & Where's Your Baby?   she
knew Last One! That's Enough! & Where's Brother
Jack?   & she was highly attuned to the
tonal modulations in J's voice   but

still   from a discipline point of view   Moll
remained a preoccupied albeit
eager to please work-in-progress   it was
not so much disobedience as sheer
enthusiasm   no elegance here

the pooch merely clumsy with vigour &
verve   zeal & zest   knocking over piles of
books   sending floor mats skidding   un-making
just-made beds   all in the desire to say
hello!   or   *hey! i just remembered i*

love you!!!   yes Moll was indisputably
filled to the brim with love   but her ways were
not always that loveable   for instance
whenever she encountered another
dog   she would immediately perform

a series of gravity-defying
bounces on all four stiffly straightened legs
accompanied by a rhythmic high-pitched
reveille (picture a fluffy feather-
duster on battery-operated

pogo sticks issuing a sound not un-
like a faulty car alarm)   over time
J realised allowing Mollie (on-
leash) to approach a given dog for a
quick sniff meant far less yipping   indeed it

was a positive social exercise
in both curiosity & constraint
but!   not all ownees welcomed an exchange
between their exquisitely behaved pooch
& the scruffy neighbourhood cur   o well

🐕

of far greater concern than the canine
encounter was the kid encounter   Moll
seemed convinced that any child between two
& six was merely A Large Dog   & that
any child at all on scooter or bike

was simply A Large Dog From Hell   these were
not 'babies' for sure!   as a mother her-
self J knew this intense conviction of
Mollie's could end (very) badly indeed
—ranger/ambulance/police—& that such

a situation must be avoided
at all cost   although Mollie had never
actually bitten anything but
a bone   J took no risks   Gentleman Jack
of course required no such measured control

J conceded how annoying it must
be to come across a barking dog—large
or small/on-leash or off—when taking a
stroll in a park   & she directed much
energy toward instilling civil

etiquette into her boisterous charge
but Moll was beyond reach   verbal commands—
Sit Down!   No!   Naughty!   Stay!—& physical
interventions (sharp tug on leash/swift slap
on back) went unheeded   frustratingly

once the dog or child had passed by   Mollie
transmogrified into picture-perfect
obedience   realising she had
misbehaved & eager for forgiveness
she would then Sit! & Stay! with absolute

monk-like focus   while J & Jack shook their
weary heads in tandem   *Mollie is of*
the great uncontrol & I am with the
significant embarrass to be of
her beside   always I am of the good

behave but the attention of Her is
of the bad behave   & the too fast &
the not listen & the don't do & the
all-thing of Mollie   & the not ever
consider the good of a being like me

apart from Dog & Child   Evil Mollie
Flanders had one more antagonist in
life   *Possum*   every evening   shortly
after sunset   an assortment of these
furry Aussie natives—ringtails/brushtails/

mothers with infants clinging to belly
or back—would begin their grand exodus
across the roof & along the cables
connecting Home to the street   cute   perhaps
but these marsupials were *loud*   making

a din on the corrugated iron
to rival a drunken football team   Moll
was not happy   hurling herself at the
balcony window   she bellowed & squealed
like a pig in a poke   J was never

quite sure what to do   let the dog onto
the balcony   where she could bark herself
senseless without ever harming a poss
(but disturbing neighbours for miles around)
or restrain her inside   where she was in

danger of throwing herself through the glass
or perishing from an acute asthma
attack   luckily the possums' nightly
migration rarely exceeded half an
hour   & by the time J had finally

decided on a course of action   it
was over   *I am of the much thankful*
when the above creatures are with the quite
complete of their activations   & I
can have the able to relax   with the

special place before the flame-box   & Her
with the doing of food in the food-place
& the girl with the sing   & the boy with
the ink-stick & paper   & Mollie at
last with the transpire to halting the yip

mollie's gonna get that noise yip! you just
watch cos that noise is mister bossy boots
stomping on our heads & mollie's gonna
get him & make him dead cos people need
to sleep & jackie boy is frightened &

i know just how to fix it all up for
everyone & it might not be tonight
& it might not be tomorrow night or
the other night but i will get him &
this is mollie's promise yip! you just watch

as well as supposedly autistic
Mollie was asthmatic   an 'autistic
asthmatic'   let's face it   J had chosen
well   there was little to be done when the
dog fell to wheezing & gasping   apart

from reciting the mantra It's okay
It's okay while stroking her back until
the attack subsided   no doubt there were
asthma medications of the doggy
kind   but there were also doggy doorbells/

toothbrushes/seatbelts/electric blankets/
bicycle sidecars/Halloween costumes/
tuxedoes/sunglasses/skateboards/footy
caps/beer/bags/shoes   where did it end?   J just
wanted her dogs to be normal   was Moll

'autistic' or *individual*   was
she 'asthmatic' or *excitable*   what
is the difference between 'lady' &
ladette   what does it matter   & as her
mum used to say   What's normal anyway?

🐕

another Christmas came & went   the dogs
had anniversaries to celebrate
in January   both having arrived
during that month   Our Brother Jack (comma)
Kerouac (full stop) had been part of the

family for six years   Evil Mollie
Flanders an eventful two   &—of course—
all three hoped there would be a multitude
of such anniversaries to come   yes
for our little trio   Life Was Good   *yip!*

🐕

Black Saturday   the day the world catches
fire   it is fifty degrees & J &
Jack & Mollie spend their hours in (& out
of) the bath   they are also bathed in a
frightening cloud of pyrocumulus

smoke   as it drifts down from J's beloved
mountain to settle in their suburb like
a fist   the sun shines through this moonscape—blood-
red   triumphant   proud—& the music of
sirens against the throbbing timpani

of helicopter blades is constant   in-
side the house   inside this day   Mollie finds
it challenging to breathe   & she adds to
the symphony as she croaks & rasps her
way through the morning   they have been warned the

evening before—high heat high winds—but
no-one really knows what to expect   J
keeps the radio on low & tries to
remain cool(ish) & calm   in between baths
she contacts W   checking her friend

is cool(ish) & calm too   both women have
been close to bushfire before   if you live
in or near the bush it is but a fact
of life   during the preceding week the
mercury refuses to leave the high

forties   only an nth of an inch of
rain has registered in Victoria
for all of January   & any
precious drop evaporates as soon as
it hits the ground   the city morgue is filled

to capacity with those succumbing
to heat-related deaths   possums fall life-
less from trees   birds from the sky   hundreds of
trains are unable to run   creating
havoc with railways buckling & twisting

& bitumen warping like dough beneath
the fat sun   random blackouts leave thousands
of households without cooling   concerts are
cancelled   even Crown Casino closes
its golden doors   keeping cool enough to

stay sane is the task   their Home is fitted
with an evaporative system   so
wonderful in so many ways—cheap to
run/clean for the environment/good for
the lungs—but under the assault of such

intense & unrelenting heat the thing
labours & is barely effective at
all   J is thus forced to cope with little
relief throughout this unprecedented
heatwave   on this day of days the house is

dreadfully hot   J feels delirious
even delusional at times   she can
not think   can not function   she finds herself
knocking against doorways & furniture
as though drunk   in their unseasonable

fur coats (which J has clipped) Jack & Evil
Moll are clearly suffering too   spending
the hours in a sleepy stupor   legs in
the air   tongues lolling   little chests rising
& falling in rhyme   she keeps bowls full of

water in every room   neither pooch wants
to venture outside   their paws burning on
the wooden porch long before reaching the
path   or the road   with much pleading J is
able to cajole them into Little

Park   but the glare of the bright dead grass is
so great—like snow!—it makes her dizzy &
they are forced Home (& this before nine in
the morning)   as the northerlies increase
to gale-force by noon on *the day the world*

catches fire   J becomes scared   the shire has
no official evacuation plan
for their residents   the choice to 'fight or
flee' left to the individual   J
smells embers & ash   burned feathers flying

above   she collects Jack & Moll & gets
back in the bath   this water is sacred
& she lifts plastic cup & gives thanks to
God & blesses their three heads again &
again & again   by nightfall J will

have lost four friends   two former Homes   & so
much of the sacrosanct bush which held her
& healed her so many times   scientists
will later compare the ferocity
of these fires to the atomic force of

400 Hiroshima nuclear
blasts   cars melted   houses vaporised   &
enormous trees were torn from the earth like
sticks   the clichés were apt   Armageddon
holocaust   horror movie   it was—yes—

Hell on earth   *I have the much scare of the*
bad-bad smell & the where   which should be with
the flame-box inside but is with the out-
side of air   & I do not have the know
for the loud-loud cry of the many noise-

with-the-fast   or the chop-chop machine with
the high above   this is most certain of
the very not-good   & I do not have
the want for the walk or the want for The
Ball   & I am with the too heat & too

scare   & I have the look of Her & I
have the look of Mollie which is with the
quite unusual   but Mollie does not
have the possess of the true understand
& at this now time   I have the do care

yip there's the yuk smell but i'm ok she's
ok jackie boy's ok even with
his sore leg so everything's ok mind
you i don't wanna breathe in all the hot
cos it hurts yip! & makes me cough & cough

but me & her & jackie stay right in
the bath & it's better & cooler than
out there cos it's bad i mean really bad
& the sounds cutting up the sky & i
don't know wot it means but yip! we're ok

J drove up the mountain one month after
the bushfires   everything she knew was gone
even the ants & the flies   it was so
quiet   she visited the church where she
was married   (gone)   she carefully trod the

remains of her first marital Home   (gone)
& later she stood in what was left of
The Shack   toed a melted saucepan   picked up
a black fork a black spoon a broken cup
& then trudged the coal-pit which had been the

beautiful bush   endeavoured to locate
that special fallen log she had sought   how
many times?   but there were too many now
& they all looked the same   she swears she would
have known it   but she did not   she did not

long story short   Hell passed   Jack & J healed
& Mollie remained herself   what a thing
this life!   there is not too much left to tell—
dear Reader—but we shall persevere   hope
for a Happy Ever After   one or

two incidents remain that just cannot
be disregarded   it was a warmish
weekday   Little Man & Moll decided
to take J for a walk   collectively
the dogs made it known their preferred port of

call was a particular area
down by the creek they had dubbed Watership
Down   scrubby   untamed   & positively
teeming with rabbits   it lay somewhat off
the beaten track   a favourite 'hunting'

haunt   especially around dusk   when each
square inch of air seemed inhabited by
a pair of long twitchy ears   though it was
only three o'clock   both pups were in the
mood   parking at the rugby field J let

Jack & Mollie run off ahead   dashing
& stopping & starting & sniffing &
darting off again   all three savouring
the sweet October breeze   when—all of a
sudden!   & out of nowhere!   there!   there!—a

bunny!   naturally the Little Man
shot off for the chase   & Moll—not really
interested—followed   how many times
had this happened before?   countless   J was
unconcerned   after the requisite few

minutes   a leaf-ridden Jack emerged from
the scrub—shame-facedly (although he had
never nabbed a rabbit in his life)—but
where was Little Girl?   J called   & waited
called   & waited   called a bit louder &

waited again   no show   how many times
had this happened before?   *never*   despite
Evil Moll's independent mind   she *loved*
owning J   *always* came to her name   this
was most unusual   so J leashed up

Jack & began to hunt   under the bridge
& behind the hall   along the creek   all
of Moll's special places   the school bell rang
& J queried the kids as they rambled
along   a black & white mutt?   a cute snub

nose?   a pink princess collar?   Sorry   &
No   so where had she got to so fast?   was
it a road?   was it The Car?   was Mollie
hiding & laughing on one of her ill-
fated larks?   the sun was sinking   this was

no longer fun   J searched & searched until
well after dark   & then she went Home   Home
with one dog   it seemed so wrong   she rang the
police/her parents/local pound   felt some
kind of peace knowing her phone number was

clearly etched into Mollie's tag   & if
someone found her   that someone would ring   but
they did not   both she & Jack felt weirdly
truncated   an essential part of them
missing   one may have thought Little Man would

be glad to regain uncontested Top
Dog status   but he did not   together
they sat on the couch   experiencing
the strange sensations of a Mollie-less
existence   *I do not have the know for*

*the now happenings   for the why Mollie
is of the not-here   I have the smell of
her at the many-creature place   & I
am of the comprehend she is near-near
to Her when she does the call   but then we*

are in the noise-with-the-fast   & Mollie
is all alone stay of that place   & I
am of the hold with the too squash in the
no-light   & the wet-face is of Her   &
I have nought of the happy of which to

apply   & I have the significant
know of the where-where of Mollie   & the
big miss of Mollie   & the much distinct
worry-worry of Mollie   but now I
have not the know or the what-what to do

𐠷

& then it began   the biggest wettest
loudest storm J had ever known   with breath-
taking force   the night sky split with strobe-like
lightning   & an ocean of thick angry
water descended amid a cracking

artillery of machine-gun thunder
& she knew   there would be no more searching
for the Little Girl tonight   J tried to
act normal   Put on pjs   Feed Little
Man   Turn on the tele   (Don't think about

Mollie)   & yes   Get into bed   but how
to sleep?   Jack had launched his terror-stricken
storm activities—crying/avoiding
her arms/endeavouring to scratch a stair-
way to heaven through the carpet/the paint

117

on the walls—completely unable to
accept any comfort from J   & the
barrage continued   Jack trapped in his own
cycle of horror   J in a strangle-
hold of grief   neither at sleep   the rain was

biblical   a vengeance!   a volcano!
a war!   it did not stop for an age or
more   tens of snaps/hundreds of strikes/thousands
of buckets of water   J wept for her
ready-for-anything daughter   out there

alone   if still alive   indeed J prayed
she *might* be dead   rather than lying all
broken in some lonely gutter   *Please God!*
Please save us! o lordy!   & then the worst
thought   J apprehended that humans can

intellectualise tempests—It's just
the weather   It won't last much longer—&
yet it was daunting   even from inside
the shelter of Home   for what of the poor
soul stuck somewhere outside?   *that was it*   with

dawn only breaking   J pulled on gumboots
& jeans &—leaving Little Man's face at
the window—jumped into car & bolted
back down to Big Park   the post-storm reserve
was still & deserted   leaves flashed silver

in the fresh pristine sun   J stood at the
spot where Evil Moll Flanders had last been
observed   & called   & waited   & called   &
waited   &—   & then—   & what was that?   the
weakest of whimpers   or was it just some

fanciful trick of the mind?   J called once
more   & there it was   the smallest of small
replies   to the creek!   Mollie? Mollie?   (*here*
here)   Mollie?!   (*here*)   J tore her way through weeds
& bracken   brambles & reeds   toward that

tiny sound   until there she stood at the
rim of the rill—now a river—swollen
& fast after last night's affair   Mollie?
(*here*)   where?   (*here*)   J peered across the rushing
water & could see nothing   nothing but

mud   where?   (*here*)   & then very slowly J
knew she could hear that the sound was coming
from mud   Mollie was part of the mud!   there
she was   a mere muddy outline   (*here*)   (*here*)
against a backdrop of mud   clearly the

creek was too risky to cross & so J
groped back up through the storm-wrecked verge   raced to
the bridge   battled through blackberries branches
& brush until there she was   directly
over the dog   but how to get down?   J

looked below at a ten-foot cliff   shiny
& smooth   & saw she could not descend   so
back to the first side again   where a washed-
away paling worked as a good makeshift
link (the *cleverest* person you ever

met!)   J tottered above rushing debris
et cetera &—yes!—she arrived at
the slim muddy bank   OMD!   where was
her rambunctious rock-rollicking punk-of-
a pup?   this was a statue of mud   Moll

(was it Moll?) just stood there unmoving   her
eyes glued shut   her legs stuck to clay   her coat
a part of the landscape   &—what a sight!—
the piece of earth the rapids had left her
was just two feet wide &—what a sight!—the

cliff wall behind her was scraped in straight lines
of desperate clawed graffiti   J picked
up the pup (who still wasn't moving) &
carried her to the car   wrapped her in a
snug woolly rug & drove her *all the way*

Home   the Little Girl was silent & still
but alive   J filled the laundry trough with
warm water   & bathed her & bathed her—five?
six times?—until the mud was gone & the
dog was revealed   exhausted & dull with

an egg on her head & bloodshot eyes   the
vet said Moll had most likely fallen down
the cliff & become concussed   was odds-on
unconscious when J had first searched   so for
the following days   poor Mollie's legs stiff

& uncertain   J took extra special
care—cuddles & blankets & hugs by the
fire—& when the pup had fully regained
her senses   she was nothing more or less
than an altogether different dog

🐕

120

when i wake up i think i'm dead & the
flashing & rain keeps bashing me up &
everyone's gone & i'm all by myself
& i wish i was home with jackie &
her but i'm not & mollie's stuck here for

ever & ever & can't get out cos
the wall's too slippery & it's too dark
& i must of been really really bad
cos mollie's alone & old mister boss
boots has eaten me up & now i'm dead

yes Mollie had changed   she was still Queen of
Fun   but that Fun was no longer as self-
serving or adolescent   she teased &
chased Jack less often   less creatively
& there existed a new inward breadth

of calm   Moll played more sedately & stayed
closer to J   especially in Big
Park   & when J spoke the Little Girl looked
her ownee in the eye   autistic?   no
way   J's canine lass merely lacked social

graces   the ability to discern
right from not-so-right   & now she had found
her place   perhaps Moll was not so much 'an
altogether different dog'   perhaps
the punk-of-a-pup had simply grown up

I have the much improvement of the like
for Mollie   example   her braveness with
the noise & the no-light   example   her
considered incredible to stay of
this life   I have the better like of her

& I have the know she has seen of the
big black   it is with her eyes   & I go
next of her for the annoy of walking
but she is no more in the spirit of
annoy   & I go next of her for the

irritate of everything   but she is
not for the irritate of all-thing at
the now   she is of the new settled &
is with the look of the significant
survive   she is of heroine to me

when J was a girl   the adults around
insisted how swiftly time passes   she
did not believe them   after all it took
all day for the sun to set & *all night*
for it to rise again   summer never

seemed to end & it felt like *forever*
before those things like Christmas or Birthday
came   but one day she knew it was true   the
mirror told her how much older   the clock
tick-tocked   & she clicked   how quickly time doth

fly   & so the years flew (at least a few)
& now—dear Reader—today has almost
arrived   what can be said?   J still had her
struggles with Dread & despair but she kept
keeping on   with Our Bother Jack (comma)

Kerouac (full stop) & Evil Mollie
Flanders right by her side   & so what of
our discussion?   (see page eighteen)   why do
we love our dogs so much?   well perhaps it
is this simple   *because the dogs love us*

dogs are animals   they are not our kin
they have four legs no arms & they wag a
tail for various reasons   dogs do not
use words but woof & yap & growl & yelp
& whine & howl & bay   they cost in terms

of money & time   they need to be walked
& washed & wormed   they are difficult &
sometimes impossible to teach   they might
bite us or slobber our new cushion or
chew our electrical cords   in certain

countries they are work-horses   in others
they are food   why—in our culture—have we
allowed the canine to become king?   what
has happened that we must elevate a
creature to such heights where it may sleep on

our bed   where we will cook it specific
food   pick up its poo   sacrifice vast sums
to fix an injured limb   invest in play-
things & minding & training   endeavour
to comprehend & cater to its strange

emotional world   & ultimately
fall into inconsolably sad depths
when it goes missing   or dies   is this love?
or simply a projection of our own
inner needs & desires?   J is not a

philosopher but she knows how she feels
& when she is greeted at her door with
real & unfailing enthusiasm
day after day   on her return from work
or a sojourn into the outside world

or when she has been absent less than two
minutes   to retrieve something from the car
or check the mail   it makes her feel good   it
makes her feel wanted & loved & good   &
when she shouts or cries or makes a mistake

she is forgiven   instantly   which makes
her feel loved   & wanted   & good   dogs don't
bear grudges   are non-judgemental   they do
not require particular high-tech or
costly environments   but when they are

provided with a few simple items
on a simple daily basis   they are
supremely content   they want to please us
by nature   they want to make us smile   it
is no complex equation   shelter plus

sustenance plus human contact equals
a cheery doggy soul   & a cheery
doggy soul is cheering to the dogged
human soul   sometimes we do not wish to
use words ourselves   sometimes all we want is

to doze & cuddle & eat & play   yes
sometimes being human is a dog's life   &
we would prefer to be a dog   even
the most complicated dogs are simple
in relation to ourselves   dogs have it

sorted   & perhaps sharing our lives with
the centredness & simplicity which
is Dog   equals the difference between
an unbearable existence & the
Good Life   which is to say Hell &/or God

at one point J savoured a one-month stay
in Cornwall   (& yes   both pooches survived)
however   while she was away a text
arrived telling her that lovely Kali—
Doggess of Destruction—had died   J could

feel W's hurt from the other side
of the earth   with her heart in pieces J's
neighbour contemplatively wrote   'Dogs know
when they want to go   they tell you with their
eyes'   & Kali—now elderly/struggling/

in pain—had told W just that   a
professional dog-breeder for many
years & ownee to multitudes over
that time   W knew how to listen
to eyes   Kali shuffled off this mortal

coil in the arms of her grieving ownee
('my Best Friend is no more')   but Kali had
sung her way throughout life like a diva
& J knew that the dog—though no Great Dane—
had been happier than Hamlet   for sure

🐕

Christmas Day & the heavens opened   no
sign of the Baby Jesus   just plagues &
plagues of unholy rain   & tons & tons
of silvery baubles which broke when they
hit the ground   ever since her trauma in

Big Park   Mollie was frightened of all things
stormy   & could no longer boast *i'm not
scared of nothing! yip!*   as the sky fractured
& the road outside became a river
she & Jack shook & shivered   while J sat

on the floor with an umbrella over
her head   yes   the tempest was tearing bits
off the roof & rudely intruding right
into their Home   this was not good   but what
could be done?   J had distributed pots

& pans to collect the spill   but now she
sat still   let everything go   let it all
just happen   she just sat there in awe   for
how many times does one get the chance to
witness such godly & ungodly might?

*I am with the distinct what-whats when the
sky does the infiltrate of Home   the wet
is of all-thing & the dry is of the
much difficult to locate   & the loud
& the crash & the brightening of all*

*around   I have the great fear but I do
the look after Mollie & Her   & hope
for the very stop soon   at least Boss Dog
is of the extra minimum   & of
fact   he has the coward run away fast*

this time i stay next to jackie & her
cos i don't wanna get swallowed up &
dead & it's nearly ok cos they are
here & mollie is not so scared of the
rain & the thunder no i'm not i'm not

morning came slowly & all at once   J
& her dogs had slept a bit & now things
were quiet up above   it was time to
assess the destruction   o lordy!   books
& carpet & cupboards & clothing quite

pregnant with water   & pieces of house
just blasted away   & they were not on
their own   neighbours with walls & roofs simply
gone   so many fridges on so many
lawns!   even the local train line had swum

off its rails   but they were okay   just like
Black Saturday   destiny?   luck?   who can
say   but J had had enough of 'weather
events'   & after a year of fixing
the place   she finally sold up   & left

J & Jack & Mollie relocated
to the coast   their new house was made of bricks
with an extra strong roof   far from firey
mountains &—fingers crossed—flood-proof   from the
very first   this Home was Dream Home   it was

of course sad to leave W although
the two friends maintained their daily emails
en français   J visited whenever
she could   it was also sad to farewell
a place where J had (mostly) been well   Our

Brother Jack (comma) Kerouac (full stop)
was now ten years old   & Evil Mollie
Flanders was six   both pooches took to life
by the sea immediately   & the
three could be found racing across sand or

swimming in shallows (Jack's 'swim' more of a
dip-your-paw paddle) or exploring the
glorious wetlands & lake   at least once
a day or more   Life—dear Reader—Was Good
(comma) Very (comma) Very (comma)

Good (full stop)   J had received a grant from
the Australia Council at last   was
relieved from the dreaded workforce for now
& days were spent writing poems like this
happily punctuated by drop-ins

from daughter (& husband) or son (& wife)
& all in an unworried domestic
domain   (yes   J had found Love again)   what
more could be asked?   J felt deeply grateful
to life   as did Moll & the Little Man

this next is of the good   & I am much
of the like for the new stay-place   & I
am not of the particular miss of
the former reside   I have specific
enjoy of my safeness beneath the small

table   from where I am of the constant
observe of Mollie & Her & Him   &
he is of the significant right   &
she is not of the wet-face so many
& I feel of the great content for my

job   I feel of the now I can do the
relax   example   the go-again with
the water of salt   but not with the huge
smash-smash & the under   no   not with the
huge but the small   & also example

the green-green & peaceful   & I am not
so much of behind that tree or around
that corner   because I am now of the
feel good safe   & I have the sense of place
for the okay for ever & ever

one could be forgiven for having thought
—given the Great Flood as well as her own
Night of Terror—that Evil Moll would be
averse to water   but the dog transformed
into a true beach babe overnight   she

loved the sea   & would leap like a gymnast
out of the car as soon as they reached the
doggy beach carpark   although it took her
a number of days to assimilate
the fact that saltwater cannot be drunk

she finally did   & then took to said
water like a fish   soaked from head to paw
& often wearing a seaweedy crown
our punk-of-a-pup would sprint across sand
& vault over rocks & harass poor old

Jack for a race   it was almost the past
Moll come back   as for Little Man   he too
loved the sea   but his interaction was
far more formal as—deep in thought—he sniffed
& snuffed his way along the shore   weighing

this with that   & content in Socratic
meanderings as long as J was in
sight   too quickly these became the good old
days   too quickly the four of them had to
re-learn what we humans always forget

yip! o yip! i love being here i love being
here with jackie boy & her & him i
just love everything everywhere cos this
is the life! there's so much to smell & see
& explore & do & i love getting

wet & racing cross the sand & jumping
on jackie & just feeling happy cos
everyone's here & mollie's ok &
even mister bossy boots is keeping
right away & everything's ok yip!

🐕

a couple of years & a couple of
books later & Jack seemed to suddenly
decline   never your true canine athlete
the Little Man began to baulk at the
stairs   & found it hard to jump in & out

of the car & up or down on/off the
couch or bed   J would throw The Ball & Jack
would just stand there   looking her deep in the
eyes *non   nein   nyet*   NO!   Jack's 'office' beneath
coffee table had become his favoured

refuge   & the dog himself turned into
a recluse inside a fortnight or so
(*non   nein   nyet*   NO!)   J was concerned for her
friend   but reasoned in her head that Jack was
simply ageing & thus bound to slowing

down   as a result walks became shorter
& cuddles got longer & everyone—
including Miss Mollie—took a little
more care of   & around   Little Man   but
his retreat continued   & so very

quickly!   until the ratter within seemed
waning away   Our Brother Jack was no
longer *Jack*   & then—   that afternoon—   when
J picked him up—   & placed him beside her—
to have a good chat—   &—   for over two

hours he carefully elucidated—
how *of the much bad* he was feeling—   how
many he loved her—   how *with the too hard*
it was to breathe—   & then J remembered
W's words   'dogs know when they want to

go   they tell you with their eyes'   (*non!   nein!   nyet!*)
(*Please God! Please God! Not yet! Not yet!*)   with heart
in throat   J drove her beloved pup to
the vet   where Jack endured test after test
with no less than pure doggy dignity

& grace   & then they were Home—   with Moll &
him & the phone—   & when it finally
rang   J-looked-at-Jack-looked-at-her   & they
knew   So sorry   (*non!*)   Lung tumour   (*nein!*)   In
pain   (*nyet!*)   Nothing to do   A week maybe

two   The best thing   (et cetera)   Leave it
up to you   Evil Moll made no move to
follow as J lifted Jack—in his *warm-
handsome-warm* tartan coat—& carried him
out to the car   & then—   to the lake   the

Little Man's most preferred place   & there they
had their last walk together   (Jack barely
able to pace ten paces   before J
perched him into *the perfect sitting for*
a being like me   his Home of twelve years   her

right shoulder)   & there they had their last talk
forever   (which—dear Reader—must remain
private)   before leaving the lake—   & then—
their last destination—   J wants you to
know   (& she finds it *much of the too hard*

to write)   that Jack entered calmly the Eighth
Elegy—   Rilke's sacred 'open'—   while
she held his head—   & whispered & whispered
Thank you—   Thank you—   Thank you sweet
    friend—   Sleep well
little buddy—   *Brave Boy Brave Boy Brave Boy*

🐈

I have the comprehend I will not be
return   I have too the comprehend that
I have loved Her   that I will always love
Her   & that at this final   love will have
all of the everything good in the end

🐈

after that—   came nothing—   & nothing lasts
for ever—   at first Evil Moll thought that
Jack would return & she was okay   but
gradually   gradually   it dawned on her
& she knew   & she mourned   & there happened

the morning when J looked & looked for the
sad Little Girl   & found her limp in her
sad little bed   face to the wall   weeping
just like you   just like me   it was the most
anguished of songs   & J gathered her up

& sang along   rocking her slowly   both
worlds altered   both hearts bereft   they farewelled
their friend together   but time heals   as they
say   & it did—   & so—dear Reader—we
finally find ourselves here   at today

🐕

it is half past four in the morning as
she writes   Moll is asleep at her feet &
somehow J knows that wherever he is
their beautiful Jack is not far away
I am having the watch of Her now   though

it is the blackness outside & she should
be at sleep   at least she is not having
the wet-face or doing the go-around
in the no-light   at least Boss Dog is of
the minimum size   & she is having

the something of happy   tapping on the
word-box   then smile   doing the stroke-stroke of
Mollie   then smile   I stay with the watch through
the many & always   it is the much
significant of my duty   & love